Fiction Agonistes

Stanford
University
Press

———————

Stanford
California

Fiction Agonistes

In Defense of Literature

Gregory Jusdanis

Stanford University Press
Stanford, California

Printed in the United States of America on acid-free, archival-quality paper

Library of Congress Cataloging-in-Publication Data

Jusdanis, Gregory, 1955–
   Fiction agonistes : in defense of literature / Gregory Jusdanis.
      p. cm.
   Includes bibliographical references and index.
   ISBN 978-0-8047-6875-7 (cloth : alk. paper)—
   ISBN 978-0-8047-6876-4 (pbk. : alk. paper)
      1. Literature—Aesthetics. 2. Literature—Philosophy.
   3. Autonomy (Philosophy) in literature. I. Title.
   PN45.J87 2010
   801'.93—dc22

                                        2009021943

Typeset by Thompson Type in 10.9/13 Garamond

Contents

	Acknowledgments	vii
	Preface: An Autobiography of the Book	1
§ 1	Overture and Themes	6
§ 2	Art's Apology	19
§ 3	Of Two Autonomies	36
§ 4	Art as Parabasis	56
§ 5	The Line Between Living and Pretending	78
§ 6	The Future of a Fiction: Or, Is There a Parabatic in the Paratactic?	101
	Notes	121
	References	133
	Index	153

Acknowledgments

If literature needs a defense, friends and family deserve acknowledgment. My wife, Julian Anderson, has gone over every line I have published with her novelist's eye. She has always encouraged me to become a better writer. Where would I be without the prodding, advice, and friendly ear of Vassilis Lambropoulos? Jim Zafris, the most literate lawyer, marked the pages with his practical pen. As a student and colleague, Ric Rader plodded through the manuscript twice, helping me stay relevant. Only a careful editor, like Jim Phelan, could be so bold in his suggestions for cutting. And how often did Roland Greene help me, though we have met only twice?

My children—Adrian, Alexander, and Clare—deserve my gratitude for having had to listen over the years to more than their share of talk about literature and the autonomous aesthetic.

Having read an early draft of the manuscript, Jochen Schulte-Sasse suggested a number of revisions. Nina Berman, Dick Davis, and Yiorgos Anagnostou provided valuable bibliographic references and explanations about key facts and ideas. Sebastian Knowles shared with me his vast knowledge of English modernism. The College of Humanities at The Ohio State University provided me with time to complete this project.

Emily-Jane Cohen of Stanford University Press proved a tenacious, well-informed editor. Sarah Crane Newman, her assistant, was prompt, helpful, and efficient. I also thank the two anonymous readers whose comments helped sharpen the argument. Margaret Pinette supervised the copyediting process with great professionalism.

I dedicate this book to my mother and late father, who, although they could not read my work, always supported it.

Fiction Agonistes

Preface

An Autobiography of the Book

Here were two grown men discussing "beauty"
seriously and with dignity as if they and the topic
were as normal topics of discussion
between men as soybean prices.
      —B. H. Fairchild, "Beauty"

I envy these men. I confess I sometimes feel at a loss when speaking about beauty. Although I can easily get hooked by a novel or film, or find myself unable to move away from certain paintings, I have often stumbled when trying to explain why this experience is important in academic language. Of course, I have come to realize that I am not alone in this dilemma. Many people have concluded that aesthetic abandon is incompatible with the gravitas of scholarly discourse. Or they allow such enthusiasm to students only. Why is this so?

We once believed that culture made us into better human beings, that we could find solutions to our problems in literature, or that art provided us with solace for the imperfections and injustices of life. I, for one, accepted these principles, like many other people before me, as my entry into bourgeois, Anglo-Saxon culture. I, too, became *"Romansfähig,"* capable of reading novels, an expression used for Jews who had become assimilated into the European Enlightenment. For many reasons, we no longer trust the justifications we learned in school of literary self-fashioning and aesthetic redemption.

Few critics or scholars nowadays agree with the central tenets we ascribe to literary humanism, namely, that the pursuit of a literary culture will produce better people. Moreover, we have lost faith in humanism's most animating feature—the compensatory powers of culture. We no longer have confidence that culture can save us or that it can offset the negative effects of modernity. To make things worse, we have not developed our own "defense of poetry," a set of arguments about the importance of literature to society. While we have deconstructed inherited justifications of literature, we have been neither willing nor able to offer others in their place at any level of education, from elementary school to university.

At the same time, the position of literature in society—always unstable—has become more precarious. Although literature has been involved in an agonistic relationship with society, this struggle has become particularly sharp in the last decades. The old class structures that supported the arts and the concomitant aesthetic ideologies are falling apart. New technologies, such as the fluid electronic writing made possible by the computer, are eroding print, which is so closely associated with literature as a public institution. Literature, like all the arts, has had to justify itself in a way not necessary before.

Many critics have celebrated this development, hailing the disappearance of literature, the collapse of culture's social autonomy, and the conversion of art into a thing among things. Others have withdrawn into a numbed silence. There are a few, however, who over the last few years have spoken up in defense of art, beauty, and the aesthetic experience.[1] These writers, inside and outside the academy, have begun to reevaluate the aesthetic and steer the discussion beyond knee-jerk condemnation and facile celebration.

My study belongs to this group, motivated by a sense that we are doing our students and ourselves an injustice by not drafting a theory of art relevant for our time. We require not retrenchment, a return to the past, but rather the reconceptualization of art's place in society that takes into account our current social situation and the theoretical questioning of the last thirty years. We do not need another attack on theory or more reverie about the world of the New York intellectuals or even the salons of nineteenth-century Paris or Goethe's Weimar. These worlds are not our own.

We have to craft our own defense of art in general and literature in particular. How else can we resist the termination of funding for the arts or, the elimination of art programs in schools, while securing the place of the Humanities in the corporate university? If we don't believe in art, why should we bother to fight against those politicians who call for the closing of controversial art exhibits? Is the only plausible case we can make the one of free speech, no matter how noble that argument is? Can we say nothing more about art? This seems like the ultimate aestheticist position, namely that art has no value other than expressing itself. It is ironic that those who have attacked the isolationism of aesthetic theories see any defense of art as ahistorical and essentialist.

It is time to move beyond this predictable reaction to the mere mention of the words *art, beauty, literature, aesthetic experience,* and *literary value*. There are many socially responsible reasons for doing this, not the least, professional survival. If we—and here I speak of myself as a teacher of literature—cannot provide our students a rationale for taking classes of literature, as opposed to those in history, geography, economics, or psychology, why should they honestly come? Can we tell them anything more than that it would make them better writers for today's marketplace, or that it is required by the core curriculum? Can't they learn how to write equally well in history, philosophy, or political science? And why are literature classes required? Many of the "practical" disciplines have no qualms about telling students why they should major in mathematics, physics, or psychology. Why do we?

My study is intended to contribute to this discussion by providing a partial answer, one based on an ancient but still vital tension in our understanding of art—the conflict between reality and fiction. I hope to reconcile two antithetical approaches: that art is an autonomous entity and that it is a social convention. What binds these strands together in my theory is the human need for simulation. When we engage in art (listening to a song, watching a film, looking at a sculpture, or reading a poem), we are conscious of entering another, invented world. Although this experience may be inherently valuable, it also sharpens distinctions we make between the real and the imaginary. I call this whetting of borders the parabatic potential of literature, a term I adapt from that part of Aristophanic comedy, when members of the chorus step forward, remove their masks, and address the audience as fellow citizens rather than as actors on the stage.

This double role of the chorus, as performers and members of the polis, highlights the dual capacity of art, to provide pleasure and a social purpose at the same time. On the one hand, we derive much enjoyment and excitement as we step into an illusory world. Yet from its fictional universe, we are also able to gaze back at the actual one, criticize it, see alternatives, or seek to transform it. In short, though we love art for its inventive potential, there is something beyond personal delight in our attraction that is political. This parabatic function underscores literature's structural relationship to reality.

But this link is not Platonic. It does not ask whether literature is truthful. The novel, for instance, may indeed aspire to be true to the world, as Myra Jehlen and James Wood have recently claimed. Literature may supply us with ways of knowing the universe. Rather than pursuing this mimetic line of inquiry, I wish to change the direction, away from objective reality to the threshold literature draws between itself and that reality. The parabatic capacity of literature illuminates the boundary separating a world of invention from the actual world.

A paradox wends through my study, namely that literature is autonomous and simultaneously socially embedded: we enjoy the execution of aesthetic form; we love particular sounds or arrangements; we take pleasure in discovering the correspondence between nature and its representation. As Wallace Stevens put it, there is "always an analogy between nature and the imagination, and possibly poetry is merely the strange dimension of that parallel" (1951: 118). At the same time, we inhabit institutions and partake in social processes: the places where we read poems, look at paintings, listen to music, and talk about works of art.

People often feel that they have to choose between these two aspects of the aesthetic experience—beauty versus place, form versus action, and pleasure versus duty. My theory of the parabatic incorporates both dimensions. It sees the imaginative world of art as the formal creation that makes sense only when compared to the real. The parabatic, therefore, is interested in this ongoing duet between aesthetic portrayal and nature, art and empirical reality, and culture and politics. If Athenian parabasis signaled the chorus's sloughing off its fictional role to criticize the politicians, the parabatic is that accordion-like divide linking actuality and its aesthetic replication.

This state of being divorced yet yoked constitutes the reality of literature. On the one hand, literature is a social institution with a long history, rooted in society and subject to political struggle and economic regulations. At the same time, it creates a cosmos in its own right, free from the denotative strictures of language, the rules of logic, and the necessity of one-to-one correspondence. Literature has leeway to construct and reconstruct the world, a freedom otherwise possible only in dreams or madness.

The ambivalence of literature is neither forced nor facile. Many thinkers through the ages have had to confront this paradox—that arts are useless and useful. "What harm is there in that?" asks Jacques, in Denis

Diderot's *Jacques the Fatalist,* when his master complains that his servant carries too many paradoxes in his head. "A paradox isn't always a lie" (1986: 64). Neither is literature. It is fiction that claims to be true. We lean on its truths.

We need literature, like the aesthetic in general, as a space where we interact with invented forms, and more important, where we experience the disparity between life and the life-like, permanence and metamorphosis. Literature is important not only because its depictions are truthful but also because it enables us to reflect on that tension between a verifiable reality and its distorted reproduction. The ability to distinguish between the actual and the imaginary is essential to us as human beings. Our capacity to imagine something new, to invent, to project ourselves into the mind of another person, and to fight for a new world is based on this distinction. The role of literature then is to highlight itself as a separate realm of human practice wherein we can imagine alternate possibilities of human relationships and political institutions.

Literature, therefore, must stand as a separate institution among other institutions in modernity. Those critics, who push for the collapse of literature into culture and culture into life, will not find support in these pages. This fusion is neither possible nor desirable. If, as I will show, poetry began to differentiate itself from other writings as early as Euripides, then we would be hard pressed to return to some Homeric organic unity, before our lapse into self-reflection.

But what type of autonomy can we now imagine for literature today when the expansive textuality of the Internet and the amphibian World Wide Web threaten to capsize the values of the book age? Certainly not the isolationism of late-nineteenth-century aestheticism. Rather I propose a complex semiautonomy where literature is both separate, as an art form, yet part of society.

Literature is a line and the breach of that line. A parabasis. It is there, yet not completely so, like the apparition of Eurydice we catch anxiously behind us, between the dead and the living, between above and below. Is it real or our imaging? And what's the difference?

§1 Overture and Themes

"Who wants poets in such lean years?"
—Friedrich Hölderlin, "Bread and Wine"

"Imagine—Greek poetry in the midst of a war."
—Constantine Cavafy, "Darius"

Do we believe that art has a place in our time? We've been hearing this irksome question for two hundred years, readers would say. And to what effect? We continue to read novels. Poetry is still published, albeit with a reduced readership. Impressionist paintings sell for millions at auction. Museums attract thousands of visitors to even less well-known traditions, such as the Byzantine or Ottoman. The Internet opens up possibilities for artistic expression. And, of course, popular culture is triumphant.

Yet, why are we silenced by art? Or rather, why are we, who study and write about the various arts, so hard pressed to defend their value? Why do concepts like beauty embarrass us? Why do we search clumsily for a rationale for what we do? We fumble for reasons that may not sound convincing any longer even to ourselves, let alone to students or the general public. In other words, although we may have a personal rationalization for the study of art (or for our preferences), we have not developed public justifications. What does art do? What are its benefits? Why should one read a novel, see a play, or go to a museum? Many of us mumble and shuffle our feet when confronted this way.

For this reason, no doubt, we don't know what to do when art is threatened by the budget cutter, the censor, or the authoritarian ruler. We experience bystander apathy. When the scythes begin to whistle in the fields of art, we look away, at a loss.

Definitions

My own study here is motivated in part by this silence. It considers the place of art in society. Because this is a vast topic, I will focus on one art, literature, with my examples drawn primarily from poems, novels, plays, and short stories. But it would not be possible to consider the fate of literature today without posing wider questions of art and aesthetics. Nor would it be historically correct to address the question of literature without also looking at previous ages, say the Renaissance or classical antiquity. Therefore, in the course of these pages I will refer to work in disciplines beyond literary criticism and to conceptions of literature in other periods.

This epistemological and historical outreach itself poses many challenges of definition. Plato and Aristotle, for instance, understand as poetry what we regard as literature. Moreover, contemporary philosophers may speak of art or the aesthetic in ways relevant to my analysis. Therefore, I will use their concepts (poetry, beauty, the aesthetic, aesthetics, and art) depending on the context, "translating" them into my own work.

Let me begin with the concept of art itself. It appeared around the eighteenth century as a means of describing the amalgamation of disparate cultural practices such as painting, sculpture, music, and poetry. These practices individually constituted separate specializations but were grouped together as a set of nonproductive, aesthetic-inducing experiences, differentiated from productive discourses.

When I speak of autonomous art, I mean a distinct sphere of human activity endowed with its own vocation. Art "participates in society by differentiating itself as a system which subjects art to a logic of operative closure—much like any other functional system" (Luhmann 2000: 133).[1] Function refers to the demarcation of art along the lines of a particular social procedure or occupation. Art, then, appears as a separate cluster of work in a society compartmentalized into autonomous domains.

The difficulty here is how to compare this modern concept with modes of aesthetic experience from previous ages. For instance, the classical Greeks did not have words for what we understand as art and literature. *Techne,* the modern Greek name for art, signified craft in ancient Greek. Although classical writers referred to painting, sculpture, and architecture as well as music, they had no broad classification for all of them. They spoke of beauty rather than art. For centuries writers used the word *poetry* to mean imaginative writing.[2]

This was true in Western Europe as well. Sir Phillip Sidney wrote a defense of poetry in 1581 (as did Shelley in 1821) rather than of literature or art. For centuries, European philosophers and poets spoke of *ars poetica*. Moreover, they conceived of poetry in terms of the Horatian formula, "to teach and to please." That is, poetry was both pleasurable and pedagogically useful. This stands in contract to modern philosophy, which presents the aesthetic experience as self-enclosed, affording satisfaction with little instrumental value.

It is important, therefore, to differentiate premodern poetics, the writing on the structure of poetry (Aristotle, Horace) and craft (Vitruvius), from eighteenth-century treatises on the sensory and affective response to beautiful objects, either natural or man-made (the Earl of Shaftesbury, Karl Philip Moritz, Immanuel Kant). Literature, for instance, indicates for us a set of genres (poetry, short stories, novels, drama) belonging to the overall category of art. It marks off a particular type of textuality (creative writing) from other domains of textual practice, such as manuals, encyclopedias, or legal briefs.[3] And it occupies distinct social niches such as the publishing house, university, newspaper, and classroom.

It goes without saying that the concepts of art and literature are historically and culturally contingent. Not only do these categories change, but also what counts as literature at any particular time varies. The popular novel of yesteryear may be celebrated as high art today. Intellectuals will wrangle whether Zane Grey westerns constitute "real" literature or whether Bob Dylan's lyrics can be studied along with T. S. Eliot or Baudelaire.

But curiously, few people touch on the issue of literature's social function. This is odd considering the host of questions burning before us: Do we have room for seemingly rarefied pastimes like poetry when so many practical concerns compete for our attention? What is the relevance of the novel, the genre that flourished in the nineteenth century to document human consciousness, in the postsubjectivity of a Facebook society? Finally, the eighteenth-century concept of the aesthetic was, if nothing else, a plea that something (a poem or a sunset) could have meaning in its own right, without recourse to other justification. If this is the case, do we then have time and space for experiences that are not productive, that don't contribute to the gross national product, that can't bring bread to the table? Finally, why do we expect students to study the arts at every level of instruction, from kindergarten to university?

The Terror of Literature

We don't have good answers because we have so little confidence in the efficacy of the arts within the public sphere. Let me provide two examples with respect to literature, one from journalism and the other from the academy. An article in the *New York Times Book Review* referred to a group of fiction writers who themselves express anguish about the ability of the novel to give voice to national catastrophe after the terrorist attacks of September 11, 2001. They wonder whether literature could represent public trauma, whether it was, in fact, capable of capturing the complexities of the modern world, a world that, as Georg Lukács wrote at the end of World War I, "no longer constitutes a favorable soil for art" (1971; 17).[4] Are people more at home with nonfiction in dark cultural moments, they ask (Donadio 2005: 27)? Do they turn to historical, geopolitical, or psychoanalytic studies instead?

These authors are registering two concerns about literature's position in the world. The first, seeing art in a struggle with action, expresses uncertainty about literature's ability to deal with horror. Other more practical modes of writing, such as history, they contend, may better explain terror and suffering. This is a surprising claim, given a three-thousand-year tradition of the aesthetic representation of political conflict from the *Iliad,* the *Song of Roland, War and Peace,* down to Tim O'Brien's *The Things They Carried.*[5] In the fight with history, art loses out. This is why the British novelist and cultural critic, Melvyn Bragg, is hard pressed to find any novels to include in his volume, *12 Books that Changed the World.* "I wanted books that I could prove had changed, rootedly, the lives of people all over the land—people on trains, people at airports, people at clubs and pubs" (2006: 321). Despite his love for *Middlemarch, Bleak House*, and *Women in Love,* Bragg can't show that these novels have effected social transformations on the lives of ordinary people. The only literary author to make the list is Shakespeare.

There is a sense that art, in a headlock with history, is bound to fall to its knees. Related to this is the fear that people prefer the sensational to beauty. The authors interviewed in the *New York Times Book Review* are anxious that the novel can't convey the frightening majesty of planes crashing into skyscrapers. The fine points of beauty are no match for the awe and dread of the sublime, as Byron understood: "Dark-heaving;— boundless, and sublime / The image of eternity" ([1812] 1936: 203). We long for enormity and inexpressibility, to be overwhelmed by magnitude. As Longinus put it, "the true sublime uplifts our souls" (1965: 107).[6]

It seems to do just that for the characters of B. H. Fairchild's "Beauty," a poem with the breadth of a novella but the formal intensity of lyric. The speaker, finding himself in front of Donatello's David in Florence, begins to think back to his youth, working in a machine shop in rural Kansas during the 1960s. What he remembers is the absence of the word *beauty* from daily vocabulary. "No male member of my family has ever used / this word in my hearing or anyone else's except / in reference, perhaps, to a new pickup or a dead deer (1998: 11)." He recalls a coworker once using this word to describe Kennedy's assassination. "Oswald, from that far, you got to admit, that shot was a beauty (14)."[7]

We want our beauty to be terrible, Fairchild seems to say. To make his point further, he alludes to James Wright's terse "Autumn Begins in Martins Ferry, Ohio," where fathers are ashamed to return home, their women are "dying for love"; their sons "grow suicidally beautiful" playing football, as they "gallop their bodies against each other's bodies" (1971: 113). We marvel at the warring vehemence of the football field, moved by its exquisiteness.[8]

What Do We Tell Our Students?

Underlying these authors' aesthetic concern is, of course, the value of literature. Commercial publishers over the past ten years have been less eager to print literary fiction. At the same time, the number of pages for fiction in high-circulation publications is dwindling. The *New Yorker*, for instance, prints fewer short stories, as does the *Paris Review*. The *Atlantic Monthly* no longer publishes fiction regularly while *GQ* has not contained any fiction since 2003 (Donadio 2005: 27). The weekly "Book Review" of the *New York Times* now publishes fewer reviews of fiction than nonfiction.[9] When asked about this, the editor argued that much more nonfiction is published than fiction (www.nytimes.com/2006/12/11/business/media/11asktheeditors). These decisions are no doubt related to the ineluctably declining interest in the literary among the general public. A survey conducted by the National Endowment for the Arts in 2004 revealed a drop in book buying, particularly of poetry, drama, and literary fiction. This downward trend is occurring among all demographic groups and regions (Weber 2004: B1).[10]

Even university presses are reluctant to support books of literary criticism. The budgetary cuts in libraries, the overproduction of books, and the unwillingness of professors to purchase the work of their colleagues, means that these presses are less keen to publish books on individual authors, unless they are canonical figures in major European languages.[11]

This structural phenomenon is related to the aesthetic silence I referred to earlier. When the children of Martins Ferry, Ohio, come to The Ohio State University, we are uncertain how to excite them about literary study. We seem confident only in giving instrumentalist reasons—that we will teach them how to write. This, according to Michael Bérubé, is the only "public rationale" that the profession can offer at the moment for itself (1998: 32, 22). To a certain extent this is fine and understandable. But is it enough? Can we find no other functions for literature that stem from its own area of expertise—the realm of aesthetic simulation and formal invention?[12]

We can get a good sense of this literary diffidence by looking at a forum on the significance of literature published in the *Proceedings of Modern Language Association* (*PMLA*). Tellingly titled "Why Major in Literature—What do We Tell Our Students?" it hangs out for all to acknowledge a row of dangling problems: waning enrollments, declining interest in literature within and outside the academy, and loss of authority to cultural studies and pop culture. Most revealing is the public admission of disciplinary self-doubt, that professors cannot explain why their students should study literature. That the question had to be posed at all, noted Carlos J. Alonso, then editor of the *PMLA,* "reflects a state of affairs removed from business as usual" (2003: 401).[13]

The situation described in the *PMLA* seems a far cry from the one represented by Tobias Wolff in *Old School,* a Bildungsroman set in a Pennsylvania private school. Arriving in autumn, the narrator finds a place enamored of literature, boys passionate about reading, eager to write poetry, and enthusiastic about the opportunity to meet Robert Frost, Ernest Hemingway, and Ayn Rand. "It tells you something about our school," the narrator says, "that the prospect of his [Robert Frost] arrival cooked up more interest than the contest between Nixon and Kennedy" (2003: 3). The pupils and teachers of the school are moved by literature in a way Plotinus thought people were stirred by beauty. Beauty, he argued, induces "wonderment and a delicious trouble, longing and love and a trembling that is all delight," leading us ultimately to a "higher love" (1992: 67). It is this "higher love" for literature that motivates so much excitement and study at the school and that constitutes part of the students' self-fashioning, how they become adults and citizens.

Today we no longer believe that literature has a substantial role to play in students' self-creation. We, as critics and professors, seem ready to abandon them to math, computers, and the natural sciences.[14] But are they not entitled to aesthetic activities, especially in a society that sacralizes work at the expense of play? If we are not sure what to tell our students about the value of literary study, what can we say to the university president or the governor about the necessity of literary study, themselves skeptical about the value of literature in comparison to utilitarian disciplines? Do we have any weapons to fight against the termination of funding to the arts in schools?

An Elegy for Art

Is literature dying, then? The complaints that people don't read fiction, that students can't understand literature, and that professors are confused about their own field seem to point to a catastrophe. Some critics have been warning of this for some time. Eugene Goodheart, for instance, refers to the "demise of the aesthetic in the academy" (1999: 26). Carl Woodring characterizes literary study as "a besieged baronial mansion" (1999: 1).[15] John M. Ellis laments the "corruption of the humanities" (1997). These critics blame our predicament on the shift in focus away from new criticism to structuralism and then poststructuralism.

Yet, even poststructuralists, like Geoffrey Hartman, bemoan today's "aestheticide," the "killing of the aesthetic dimension of art of life" (2002: 220). Harold Bloom worries about "the flight from the aesthetic among so many in my profession" (1994: 16–17). The indictment of literature by academics, George Levine writes, can only lead to the conclusion that to teach literature is to enumerate injustices and mistakes of western culture (1994: 16). This is so because, for a significant number of scholars, "the recent theoretical revolution has made the term 'aesthetic' and the cluster of ideas it contains outmoded and irrelevant" (Elliott, Caton, and Rhyme 2002: 9). If they don't know what to tell their students, Isobel Armstrong believes, it means they have abandoned analysis of the aesthetic experience to conservative thinkers (2000: 5).[16]

Of course, reports of art's death have been overstated for many decades. Philosophers began to mourn art's death paradoxically the moment it emerged as a social entity in the eighteenth century. Although this elegiac tradition goes back to Johann Joachim Winckelmann, it is associated with Hegel who gave it magisterial expression in lectures delivered during the winter of 1828–29 at the University of Berlin. Hegel argued that modern art "is the self-transcendence of art but within its own sphere and in the form of art itself" ([1835] 1975: 80). Art came to an end with the appearance of absolute self-knowledge; it became a philosophy, preoccupied with what constitutes art. Or, as Arthur C. Danto put it with respect to twentieth-century art, "all there is at the end *is* theory, art having finally become vaporized in a dazzle of pure thought about itself, and remaining . . . solely as the object of its own theoretical consciousness" (1986: 111).[17]

Hegel's thesis on art's demise had two components. First, when art emerged as a differentiated field in its own right, it had necessarily cut itself off from society. Like Winckelmann and Friedrich Schiller before him, Hegel believed art had reached its most exalted stage in classical antiquity because it was organically rooted in its environment, a link severed in modernity. This is why Hegel wrote that the "beautiful days of Greek art, like the golden age of the later Middle Ages, are gone" ([1835] 1975: 10). Modern art—art conscious of itself as artifice—no longer counts for people as the highest existence of the spirit. Cut off from life, it cannot meet their spiritual wants.

Hegel believed that we have killed art by turning it into an object of philosophical inquiry. When we subject art to "intellectual consideration" about its contents and modes of representation, he wrote, it no longer arouses in us satisfaction but rather our judgment. "The *philosophy* of art is therefore a greater need in our day than it was in days when art by itself as art yielded full satisfaction. Art invites us to intellectual consideration, and that not for the purpose of creating art again, but for knowing philosophically what art is" ([1835] 1975: 11). While Greeks may have enjoyed and used art as part of their lives, we separate it from our daily concerns, placing it at arm's length in galleries.[18]

For all its insight, however, Hegel's view of Greek art idealizes Greek culture. Poetic writing actually began to separate itself from other forms of linguistic practice around the fourth century BCE, if not the fifth. Aristotle, for instance, distinguished the beautiful from the theory of being. Moreover, something akin to the eighteenth-century notion of literature appeared in the fourth century BCE, when song was examined apart from other cultural discourses. The idea emerged at this time of "literature" as an artful writing with special value. Isocrates (436–338 BCE), for example, challenged the inherited conception of poetry as containing valuable knowledge or leading to metaphysical truth. This laid the basis for Greeks to see poetry ultimately as no longer speech in meter but as imaginative composition (Ford 2002: 250). Furthermore, a theory of genres evolved that dictated to each form topics, language, and musical devises. These phenomena culminated in the academic criticism of the Hellenistic Age, the first professionalized practice devoted to the study of literature, when critics began to isolate the literary and challenge its hieratic and didactic claims, in short, a process analogous to modern developments.

So the death-of-art thesis seems to mourn two phenomena: the actual appearance of art as a social institution detached from social life and paradoxically the collapse of this autonomy. It goes without saying that this discourse has been entangled with the greater story of apocalypse—the end of history—an idea that has meandered from Hegel to Antoine Augustin Cournot, to Oswald Spengler's *The Decline of the West* (1926–28), to Alexandre Kojève, and most recently to Francis Fukuyama's *The End of History and the Last Man* (1992).[19] Central to this view is that the West, no longer capable of sustaining its own "Imperium Romanum," is left with cultural fatigue—Verlaine's decadence and Cavafy's neurasthenic souls waiting for the barbarians. Of course, those who lament the passing of the aesthetic today are concerned less with Spengler's ethical lethargy than with the possible demise of art.

What do these writers mean by this sensationalist phrase, the death of art? Obviously not physical destruction of museums or books. Rather they have two processes in mind: (1) the collapse of an evolutionary, linear view of art history and (2) the possible extinction of particular arts, such as lyric or the novel.

The first has to do with the waning of a particular historical narrative that saw human society as tending toward fulfillment and amelioration. Gradually receding today is the Kantian notion that history is an inevitable process, guided by "Nature's secret plant" to bring forth a "perfectly constituted society," a "universal cosmopolitan condition" (Kant [1784] 2001: 21, 23).[20] For art, this means we are seeing the demise of a teleological story—its unfolding drive toward the new, of the perennial expectation of the avant-garde, the future as novelty (Belting 1987: 3).

The second concerns the disappearance of particular art forms, such as literature, either because they have exhausted possibilities of formal innovation or because they have lost their audience. Critics point to the following developments: (1) The explosion of culture into popular forms—through advertising, canned music, fashion—which undermine the separation of the aesthetic from other spheres. (2) The appearance of competing media such as video, the Internet, and hypertext, which challenge the dominance of print and the autonomy of literature. (3) The fading of the high bourgeoisie, the supporter and consumer of this art, and the consequent loss of its cultural influence.

There is plenty of evidence for this, as I have mentioned. Novels are less likely to be seen as templates of national identities in the twenty-first century. Literary texts do not enjoy the same privileged position in the schools of Europe or North America. Reading literary fiction or lyric poetry does not constitute an important task, even for most elites. A transformation is taking place of the modern construct of literature, the body of writing, which flourished in capitalist society between the 1750s and 1950s, and which was made possible partly by print. In our postindustrial, postprint society, literature may increasingly appear "less and less a fact of nature and more and more a single episode in a much longer history of letters in western society" (Kernan: 1987: 283).

What may be disappearing are not works themselves—*Epic of Gilgamesh*, the *Shahnameh*, "Othello," *Gulliver's Travels*, "Faust," "Kubla Khan," "The Flowers of Evil," *Crime and Punishment*, *Ulysses*, "Waiting for the Barbarians," *Omeros*, or *One Hundred Years of Solitude*—but the way we organize and read them. For this reason I propose we move beyond the celebration of or mourning over art's death, avoiding the language of the *Götterdämmerung* and of the sack of Troy and recast the situation as a transition. Although we, as intellectuals, cannot undo technological and social changes around us, we can conceive of an argument for the occupation, enjoyment, and study of art.

A Storied Existence

Let's stop worrying about whether the novel will exist in one hundred years and consider instead why people read fiction in the first place. Of course, the novel appeared in various societies for a host of complex reasons: the rise of print, the creation of reading publics, the effects of nationalism, and the increased leisure time among women. But deep down the novel is a story, and human beings take pleasure in telling and hearing narratives as they do in distinguishing between real events from their aesthetic representation.

Ellen Dissanayake goes so far as to offer a biological explanation of the aesthetic, claiming that art is part of our organic makeup and thus essential to our survival (1992: 33). Whether the arts have served as adaptive mechanisms (92) or not, it is hard to deny that they have historically been associated with ritual, rites of passage, conviviality, and war. The capacity to respond to beauty may be as human as the desire to engage in play. People all over the world react to color, rhythm, pattern, and repetition; they value sound, movement, and decoration. These processes are part of our shared nature.

In *The Literary Mind*, Mark Turner helps us understand our capacity to distinguish objects and events and then to combine them into small spatial narratives as part of our evolutionary development (1996: 14).[21] The creation of a story is a "fundamental instrument of thought," as strong as our motivation for color vision or sentence structure (4–5). Turner describes the mind as literary because it constantly fashions narratives and then projects them onto other narratives. We imagine reality and construct meanings through processes that are literary. Stories are our Lego blocks. The most sophisticated works of literature are built on them.

Narrative structures, Anthony Paul Kerby writes, are indigenous to human existence rather than an imposition of art upon life. Our understanding of ourselves is that of a character in a story (1991: 12). When we speak about ourselves we relate to episodes and points in a plot. Kerby echoes here Alasdair MacIntyre's view that "we all live out narratives in our lives and . . . we understand our own lives in terms of the narrative that we live out." Humans are story-telling animals and life has an essential "narrative unity" (1981: 197, 201, 212).

This research into the storied nature of human existence echoes the work of early aestheticians into the constitutive role of play. Finding an intricate relationship between our engagement with play and our appreciation of beauty, these writers strived to demonstrate the centrality of art in life. Schiller, for instance, viewed the play-drive as a union of the form-drive and the material-drive, mind and matter, defining play as the center of "man's states and conditions" (1967: 103, 104). "Man only plays when he is in the fullest sense of the word a human being, and *he is only fully a human being when he plays*" (107). This is why, he felt, that "beauty is not degraded by being made to consist of mere play and reduced to the level of those frivolous things which have always borne this name" (105). He pointed to Greek art and Olympic contests that exemplified the union of play and beauty, earnestness and art.

Similarly, the Dutch cultural historian, Johan Huizinga proposed a direct relationship between play and the aesthetic. More than a physiological phenomenon or a psychological reflex, he saw play as basic to the way previous societies understood poetry and art. Antique poetry was a fusion of play and words, ritual and entertainment, artistry and riddle making, persuasion and competition ([1944] 1980: 120). All poetry derived from play: "the sacred play of worship, the festive play of courtship, the martial play of contest" (129).

But are these evolutionary arguments enough? On the one hand, they are an important corrective to our social and political justification of literature. There is more to literature than the creation of female subjectivities and national identities. At the same time, literature, like the other arts, builds on basic drives and instincts, becoming a public edifice in its own right, not reducible to human impulses. In the course of history, the arts have developed social meanings and structures that extend beyond the human recognition of color patterns or the construction of narrative. Knowing their biological origins does not free us from having to analyze this historical development and ask whether this institution is relevant today.

Thus, I use these universalist arguments above only as a starting point. I am not interested in a Kantian exercise to determine the global validity of literature—to identify the mental features that permit all people to respond to literature. I propose instead to look at both the historical emergence of literature and its future purpose. Although my conception of literature, as a parabasis, may have its roots in the human capacity to distinguish truth from fiction, my aim is to examine the fate of literature as a social form.

The Beauty of Truth

My conception of the parabatic is an attempt to revisit the old tug-of-war between beauty and truth. Few critics now, for instance, would embrace Keats's (1795–1821) celebratory phrase, "beauty is truth, truth beauty" from "Ode on a Grecian Urn" (1966: 243). Nor would they describe the current situation of art with Heidegger's language. "Is art still an essential and necessary way in which that truth happens which is decisive for our historical existence," he asks, "or is art no longer of this character" (1971: 78)? Since we don't think of art as revealing truth, we don't believe it is "decisive" for our lives. But how can we put the matter then in ways that are relevant to us?

One could, of course, try to reverse the way we see art, and argue, like the Portuguese poet, Fernando Pessoa, that poetry is more truthful than practical disciplines. "Newton's binomial theory is as beautiful as the Venus of Milo. / The fact is, precious few people care" (1982: 126). One of the characters in Tom Stoppard's play, "Voyage," says something similar.[22] Trying to explain Schelling's notion of the cosmos as nature struggling toward consciousness to Michael Bakunin's sisters, Nicholas Stankevich asks them to think about the concept as a poem or a picture. "Art doesn't have to be true like a theorem. It can be true in other ways" (2002: 16–17).

Pessoa and Stoppard believe that art constitutes its own cosmos, governed by its own laws. That it should not be judged by principles outside of its domain where it is bound to lose has been a standard way of justifying art's independence from social laws. Art does what it does and cannot be held to principles outside of its sphere. Useful as this argument is, I think we need to move beyond this nineteenth-century definition of autonomy because it denies art's social context.

Art, as a social phenomenon, has consequences that aesthetic experiences do not or are not expected to have. Strolling through the park, smelling a gardenia, having dinner with the family, stroking a purring cat on our lap, or watching a fireworks display may all be valid pastimes. We engage in them simply for their pleasure. We can partake in a conversation with a friend for its sake rather than for an instrumental purpose. We may like hearing her voice, watching her stroke her hair as she speaks, or hearing her news while she glances at us. We get similar joy from observing the grace of a dance, the symmetry of a face, or the formal qualities of a poem.

But art, as institution, is different. Not just a personal pastime, it is a social praxis with public affects, autonomous yet rooted in society, claiming to be truthful while being fictive. We, therefore, have to devise theories that recognize art's autonomy but also demonstrate its social impact. A hint of this is offered by Ezra Pound in "Hugh Selwyn Mauberley": "As for literature / It gives no man a sinecure" (2003: 254). Literature does not promise carefree employment. But it does do something; it has social consequences. Figuring out what that "it" and "consequences" are, remain the challenge.

§2 Art's Apology

"There is something wrong somewhere in our social formulas."
—E. M. Forster, *Howards End*

In Anton Chekhov's novella, *Three Years*, three characters chat about the central problem affecting literature—its relevance in a time of specialization and ends-driven thinking. If literary writing promotes a separate truth, what validity does this truth have? Yulia, the wife of the protagonist, Alexei Laptev, considers the definition of literature with Laptev's two friends, Kostya and Yartsev. A work is significant, Yartsev says, when it treats serious social problems. He, therefore, dismisses novels without lofty themes. Agreeing with him, Yulia adds, "There are so many people who are sick, unhappy, and worn out by poverty: to them such [trivial] books must be revolting" (1960: 184). Yartsev protests, however, arguing if poetry did not answer to questions that seem "important to you, you ought to consult books on technical subjects, criminal and financial law; read scientific pamphlets." Then he reveals his instinctive understanding of art's role in a compartmentalized society where each sphere defines its own occupation: "What would be gained, if, say, in *Romeo and Juliet*, they had a discussion about freedom of speech or the disinfection of prisons, when you can find everything on the subject in special articles and manuals?" (184). The American fiction writer, Charles Baxter, would agree. "Sometimes readers are not going to be helped along by the stories they read. Literature is not an instruction manual" (1997: 76–77). Literature is neither revelation nor treatise, but something altogether different.

Although separated by more than a century, both Chekhov and Baxter insist on the legitimacy of literature's autonomy; its claims to truth have their own validity. That Baxter himself has to assert this shows that we are still grappling with the same questions. What can art do in a functionally differentiated society where each domain has a specialized task? Does it imitate other disciplines, appropriating their expertise? Or does it exploit its own special capacities, promoting its own unique tasks? Can it compete with practical discourses on their own territory? Or will it be made redundant and cast aside?

Chekhov and Baxter confront a paradox that tears through our understanding of literature. On the one hand, they declare its freedom but, on the other, they have to deal with the consequences of this sovereignty. Can literature, as one specialized mode of human practice, speak to a wider public? What is the role of a "useless" discourse in society that celebrates efficiency, work, and the practical application of ideas? These questions point to the troubled place of literature today.

This tenuousness stems primarily from literature's functional differentiation. That is, it has become more vulnerable because of its structural position where it exists as one but no longer revealed discourse. Its capacity to speak about the world has limited validity beyond its own tautological self-validation. But it would be inaccurate to suggest that literature's place was secure before its autonomous configuration. As a mode of writing dealing with illusions, literature has always been vulnerable, the object of suspicion and attack. Russell Fraser speaks of a general "war against poetry" waged through the ages (1970) while Arthur C. Danto has referred to the "philosophical disenfranchisement of art" (1986: 7). Literature has always seen itself as an agonist involved in a contest.

However we choose to characterize this fight, the aggressor has defined the terms, be they made on philosophical, historical, scientific, or technological grounds. The struggle is played out, in the words of M. H. Abrams, "on terrain selected by the opposition" (1958: 2), using the criteria of morality, efficacy, instrumentality, and action. Poetry, meanwhile, has asked to be judged on intrinsic criteria. Or as Shelley puts it, "the jury which sits in judgment upon a poet . . . must be composed of his peers" (1890: 11). This not being the case, poetry has lost these rounds over the centuries.[1]

The Attack on Poetry

In order for us to understand literature's predicament today, we have to come to terms with the "warfare" against poetry declared first by Plato.

In the first section (Book III) of the *Republic* Plato was concerned with the education of the commonwealth's "Guardians," specifically the selection of appropriate "literary" material for this purpose. He found that the staple of pedagogical texts—Homer, the lyric poets, the dramatists—was unsatisfactory because they were either engaged in falsehoods or disrespectfully represented the divine: "Then we must not only compel our poets, on pain of expulsion, to make their poetry the express image of noble character; we must also supervise craftsmen of every kind and forbid them to leave the stamp of baseness, license, meanness, on painting and sculpture, or building, or any other work of their hands" ([III 401] 1945: 90). He also banished poetry for its lack of expertise. In the famous section of Book X concerning the "quarrel between philosophy and poetry," Plato wrote that "all poetry from Homer onwards, consists in representing a semblance of its subject" ([X 600] 331). Thus poets do not have the knowledge to educate people "and make them better men" ([X 600] 330). Plato strived to show poetry's inadequacy to explain and represent reality because poets claimed to "understand not only all technical matters but also all about human conduct" ([X 598] 328–29).[2] He voiced the fear of poetry's hubristic claim to explanatory potential beyond its expertise.

Aristotle countered Plato's rejection of poetry by proposing that it was more philosophical than history. Poetry's function, he explained in the *Poetics* (1984), was to describe, "not the thing that has happened, but a kind of thing that might happen." Poetry was superior in that "its statements are of the nature rather of universals, whereas those of history are singular" (2323 [1451b1]). Furthermore, Aristotle treated poetry as a valid object of philosophical analysis and introduced the intrinsic method of textual study:

> I propose to speak not only of poetry in general but also of its species and their respective capacities; of plot required for a good poem; of the number and nature of the constituent parts of a poem; and likewise of any other matters in the same line of inquiry." (2316 [1447a10])

Despite Aristotle's formalist approach, poetry had to adopt a self-protective posture, forced to defend its existence vis-à-vis history and philosophy. This has been the central dilemma of poetry: to justify itself by claiming expertise outside its realm but then stand accused of appropriating undue authority. Poetry has always had to confront a skeptical tribunal that either dreaded its power or condemned it for being powerless.

Responses to this tribunal, Margaret W. Ferguson shows, have taken the form of "apology, defense, excuse, or justification, types of discourse that presuppose the existence of an accusation" (1983: 1).

In the Renaissance, this apologia constituted a genre that explored the boundaries between speech and writing. Authors of these texts were involved in a conflict over the values of labor and leisure and specifically over which activities belonged to each category (Matz 2000: 1). They conceived of their defense of poetry in terms of the Aristotelian and Horatian tradition that considered poetry a didactic discourse.[3] Sidney, for instance, defined poetry as an "art of imitation" whose end was to "teach and delight" (101). The superiority of poetry lay in its capacity to teach virtue while being enjoyable. In addition to this, however, Sidney strived to demonstrate that poetry motivated, rather than weakened, military valor. By its pleasures, poetry could guide men toward virtue. Sidney linked poetry and politics when he wrote that poetry is a "companion of the camps" (1965: 127–28). In short, the Renaissance poet wished to "lead people to act on the idea of virtue represented in the poem" (Clark 2000: 4).

Poetry's defensive stance has intensified in modernity as art has developed into a separate domain of social practice. The processes of functional differentiation have undercut poetry's universalism, which Aristotle held as its quintessential feature. In modernity every art specialized in one function. Art in a sense answered Plato's accusation—that "the artist knows nothing worth mentioning about the subjects he represents" ([X 601] 1945: 332–33)—by making artists professionals, speaking only of their skills. Each art, as Gotthold Ephraim Lessing argued (1965) in his *Laocoön*, sought its own purity by exploiting its own intrinsic elements.[4]

Differentiation, however, rendered the position of art more doubtful than before. Art's specialization highlighted its worthlessness at a time when it was subjected to the market's principles of efficiency and rationalization. Schiller expressed the predicament in *On the Aesthetic Education of Man*: "Utility is the great idol of our age, to which all powers are in thrall and to which all talent must pay homage. Weighed in this crude balance, the insubstantial merits of Art scarce tip the scale" ([1795] 1967: 3). Focused on its specialized occupation, uncertain about its ecumenicity, less capable of influencing society than religion or schooling, art seemed to have lost its value. This is why, Hegel believed, it had become necessary to defend the arts "in their relation to practical necessities in general, and in particular to morality" (1975: 4).

The defense of poetry and art took on a more passionate tone in Shelley's "A Defense of Poetry" (1890). Like Sidney, Shelley claimed that poetry was superior to philosophy because poetry actually "creates new materials of knowledge, and power, and pleasure." Moreover, poetry is at the "center and circumference of knowledge; it is that which comprehends all science, and that to which all science must be referred" (38). Poetry, in short, constitutes its own world, creating fictions that claim to be true. These arguments, however, could no longer convince readers of poetry's occupation as they had done in Sidney's time, not because they had less vigor but because literature, as only one art among others, justified itself on the basis of its autonomy. Its epistemological claims were more circumscribed.

The old question about the relationship of fictionality to truth took on a different twist when literature could offer only specialized discourse about invention. In other words, while people still remained distrustful of literature, the reasons for their distrust changed when literature became a self-sufficient institution. The modern critique of art, therefore, has to do with its autonomy (lack of sympathy for the world) rather than with mimesis (lack of truth), as was the case in antiquity. Rather than holding art up to a mirror and finding its reflections deficient, we accuse it of withdrawal from history into its own isolation. [5]

Art and Justice

Walter Benjamin expressed this tendency when he pointed to the contradictions between the gleaming edifice of cultural monuments and the misery of the ordinary people who produced them. These treasures, Benjamin wrote, "owe their existence not only to the efforts of the great minds and talents who have created them, but also to the anonymous toil of their contemporaries." Then Benjamin added what has become one of his most quoted pronouncements. "There is no document of civilization which is not at the same time a document of barbarism" (1969: 256). Or, as Bertold Brecht asked in his poem, "Questions from a Worker who Reads":

Who built Thebes of the seven gates?
In the books you will find the names of kings.
Did the kings haul up the lumps of rock?
And Babylon, many times demolished
Who raised it up so many times? (1976: 252–53)

Responding to the uncritical celebration of culture, Benjamin and Brecht have forced us to confront a truth that over the ages people have easily ignored: Beauty has been tainted by empire, slavery, and class structures. Although the realization of this contradiction did not prompt Benjamin or Brecht to abandon art, it certainly has done so among a host of critics, particularly after the 1960s. For decades, Elaine Scarry notes, people have "either actively advocated a taboo on beauty or passively omitted it from their vocabulary" because they think it either distracts our attention from injustice or because it objectifies reality (1999: 117, 58).[6]

These writers have shown that the frieze in the temple of culture has glossed over stories of genocide, slavery, political repression, and poverty. Although high culture can heighten personal sensibilities, it can also enforce class divisions. Taste, the acquired disposition to differentiate and appreciate cultural goods, is also a process of distinction by which individuals identify and solidify their social position. This enhanced faculty of perception at the same time helps to locate these groups on the social ladder (Bourdieu 1984: 28).

No one who works within the realm of culture, especially one wishing to defend art, can ignore these contradictions. There is a tension between the ideal of a democratic art and the reality of its exclusivity, between demotic discourse and elitism. This conflict between the purported universality of culture and the limits to its realization has often been the subject of literature, most poignantly perhaps in Thomas Hardy's *Jude the Obscure* ([1895] 1998). On the one hand, the novel recognizes its own aesthetic autonomy, exploiting the conventions and formal modes of Victorian fiction. It also sees itself as a participant in wider struggles, by bringing to light the social injustices confronted by the protagonist who wishes to succeed in the game of culture. The novel thus illustrates the theory I develop in the later chapters that literature is both a site of simulation and a means to recognize the difference between simulation and reality.

Jude is the painful example of a man who seeks inclusion, who desires the satisfaction promised by the pursuit of culture, who hopes to distinguish himself through art. Yet, the towers of Christminster, Hardy's fictional Oxford, remain inaccessible to him. He has neither the social nor financial capital for entry. Hard work as a mason in Christminster grinds him down. Not able to reach his goal, he abandons the city, a broken man.

Years later upon his return to Christminster with his entire family, he runs, while watching a college procession, into fellow masons with whom he worked in the city. They mock him both for his ambitions and his failure. His response, at once guileless and self-pitying, reveals the injustices of the system:

> However it was my poverty and not my will that consented to be beaten. It takes two or three generations to do what I tried to do in one; and my impulses—affections—vices perhaps they should be called—were too strong not to hamper a man without advantages; [. . .] You may ridicule me. [. . .] But I think if you knew what I have gone through these last few years you would rather pity me. And if they knew—he nodded towards the college at which the Dons were severally arriving—it is just possible they would do the same. ([1895] 1998: 326)

It is doubtful that the dons would ever notice him amid the majesty of the day. They do not register his catastrophe, like the peasants in Pieter Breugel's painting "The Fall of Icarus" (1558), who carry on with their plowing, cruelly unaware of the youth's plunge into the sea. His struggles to transform himself remain, as suggested by the novel's title, obscure. "There is something wrong somewhere in our social formulas," Jude protests (327). His life, he acknowledged, is a "moral story" of a man who tried but fell short.

Yet, Jude's failure is also primarily the failure of culture widely and of the novel, as an art form, particularly. Does the novel itself not contribute to the social exclusion it portrays? Its plea for verisimilitude is underwritten by aesthetic autonomy. In other words, its claim to representational truth is made possible not by the bardic qualities of poetic language but, more narrowly, by the conventions of nineteenth-century realism. It aspires to depict through the customs of fiction, rather than the practical language of sociology or history. The processes of self-refinement and education, necessary to enjoy the novel as art, prevent Jude from entering culture the novel represents. Yet, while reality excludes Jude, fiction includes him in its aesthetic enactment.

Fifteen years later, E. M. Forster's *Howards End* stages similarly subtle processes of cultural ostracism. The ultrasophisticated Schlegel sisters, Margaret and Helen, who are of German descent, feel themselves distant from the mercantile and culturally unrefined Wilcox family. This gap is particularly made apparent when Helen, upon her return from a visit to the Wilcox household, begins to enumerate the differences between the two families: They find her notions of life "sheltered and academic";

they consider socialism and feminism "nonsense," they even regard her understanding of literature and art as babble "when not conducive to strengthening the character" (1999: 22).

The Schlegel sisters are social snobs, triumphant in their cultural sophistication and exultant in the distinction both bring about. This is borne out by Margaret's reaction to the unexpected visit from the *kleinbürgerlich* Leonard Blast, who would eventually marry her sister. Observing him as she descends the stairs, Margaret concludes that he looks like a "grandson to the shepherd or ploughboy whom civilization had sucked into the town, as one of the thousands who have lost the life of the body and failed to read the life of the spirit" (105). Leonard seeks inclusion in the life of culture, but the liberal Margaret is of a different mind. "Culture had worked in her own case, but during the last few weeks she had doubted whether it humanized the majority, so wide and so widening is the gulf that stretches between the natural and the philosophic man, so many the good chaps who are wrecked in trying to cross it" (105). There could be no more candid portrayal of the inconsistencies inherent in both cultural ideology and liberalism. Margaret finds it difficult to accept someone like Leonard, who works as a clerk in the Porphyrion Fire Insurance Company and who knows only "the outsides of books." While Margaret does not seem as brutal and absolute to Leonard as the nameless dons are to Jude, her thoughts demonstrate the nuanced way culture may be employed as a class barrier.

In demonstrating this process so openly, the novel also affects its own marginalization. For by showing that the acquisition of culture is a project of self-fashioning, that Matthew Arnold's "study and pursuit of perfection" ([1869] (1971: 58) is acquired at home and at school, it brings attention to its own role in social exclusion.[7] That the real Leonards and Judes have been thwarted in their efforts to find self-fulfillment through high culture is after all one of the reasons that people renounce art. Both novels here dramatize the parabatic capacity of literature. The issue is less whether these characters have "lifeness" (Wood 2008: 247) than that their fictional representations invite us to compare the real and the imaginary, to take pleasure at the formal invention, and then to rebuke social injustice.

The Allure of Aestheticism

Critics often ignore literature's role in spotting life's wrongs, concentrating on its aestheticism. To be sure, aesthetic autonomy can lead to a validation of form as form and the glorification of art as the supreme manifestation of life. Literature itself is alert to this very threat. The reader of one of Stephen's essays in *Stephen Hero* (the first draft of *A Portrait of the Artist as Young Man* that Joyce nearly destroyed) fears this, arguing that "this theory you have—if pushed to its logical conclusion—would emancipate the poet from all moral laws" and lead to art for art's sake (1977: 88). Although Stephen states earlier that "art is not an escape from life," he realizes that modernist theory could come to celebrate the superiority of art over life, elevating its power to affect social reality.

Aesthetic autonomy can slide into aestheticism: while art appropriates responsibility over its own domain, it aspires to apprehend life, becoming itself life. Having fended off the pressures of reality by creating fiction, it purports that we know reality better through form. The reality of form becomes truer than the reality of the senses. Or so it claims.

We have come to distrust these aestheticist assertions. We fear not only that appreciation of form might make us blind to misery around us—Aschenbach's fascination with the exquisite Tadzio during the plague in Venice—but also that it may reduce politics and economics to matters of beauty—Oscar Wilde's elevation of art as the supreme good. Rather than being a beacon that highlights conceptual and social differences—as was the case of *Jude the Obscure* and *Howards End*—the aesthetic could turn into a cauldron that melts distinct categories such as object and subject, reason and emotion, analysis and appreciation, language and reality.

This is why for many critics aestheticism "is certainly a risk whenever a theory deals with questions of art and literature"; they approach it with "distrust" (Carroll 1989: xiii). Some theorists, like Terry Eagleton, recognize the ambivalent nature of the aesthetic: it "figures as a genuinely emancipatory force" but it also signifies a kind of "internalized repression" (1990: 28). On the one hand, the aesthetic helps to unfetter individuals from society. It creates a new human subject, one who could challenge political authority (28). With its emphasis on personal autonomy, the aesthetic offers a different model of agency, according to which society is constructed rather than divinely inspired, and hence capable of being changed. The autonomous individual is the one who believes in and fights for political self-determination at home and later in the colonies.

On the whole, though, critics have not been kind to the aesthetic in the last thirty years. Even Eagleton himself describes it, more often than not, as a conservative ideology, promoting social order through the idea of

"spontaneous consensus." A range of writers from Marxists to deconstruc-
tionists have written about the dangers and allure of the aesthetic: from
Raymond Williams, who sees the aesthetic as "main instrument" of social
"evasion" (1977: 154), to Paul de Man, who regards it as a creole concept
that confuses knowledge with aesthetic judgment, ethical understanding
with desire, reason with morality, yielding ultimately not the exact apprehension of the world but one that is "polluted" (1984: 137–38; see also
de Man 1986).[8]

Critics denounce the aesthetic because of its potential to seduce us, to
mix categories, to muddy borders between thought and practice, a fear
that was shared by modernist artists themselves who associated it with
feminine allure, messiness, and dependence (Steiner 2001). For many
writers, the aesthetic, having withdrawn within its own fort, now strikes
out with a phalanx of tropes.

Breaking of Boundaries

Critics react to this formal expansion in two seemingly contradictory
ways. On the one hand, they want to detonate art's separate space and to
return it back to nature. On the other, they contend that art has already
exploded into tiny pieces and thus has been reintegrated with society.

Let me turn to the first claim. Because intellectuals have often interpreted art's compartmentalization variously as its escape from history,
its evasion of ethical responsibility, or its indifference to suffering, they
have sought to weaken art's autonomy by denying it special status. They
celebrate postmodernism, for instance, as an "anti-aesthetic" discourse,
repudiating Kantian aesthetics (Bohls 1995: 22). This would presage pre-
sumably the return of art to its previously undifferentiated mode, that
is, its effective disappearance as a formal entity. Mark C. Taylor looks
forward to such an event, contending that art will die when it becomes
indistinguishable from other forms of cultural production (2001: 8).
Similarly, Rei Terada believes we should strive to make literature a thing
among things. Writing on the teaching and meaning of lyric today, she
asks us to let "'lyric' dissolve into literature and 'literature' into culture,
using a minimalist definition of 'culture' from which no production or
everyday experience can be excluded" (2008: 199).

Sociologically, such folding of art into the wider social world would
constitute what theorists refer to as dedifferentiation, the opposite

of functional differentiation, that is, the breaking of borders between spheres and their consequent merger. But what does it entail? What will we do with the arts once they lose their autonomy? Are we going to wear them? Worship them? Use them to justify imperial power or glorify the president?[9] Incorporate them into religious or political festivals? Employ them in legal proceedings? These were some of the uses the arts have been put to in the past. In short, what exactly would it mean *now* to make a poem, a piece of music, or a painting a thing among things? Will we disband galleries, concert halls, or theaters? Will we display sculpture in natural history museums along with shells and rocks? Or will we judge a poem by its practical or moral value?

Moreover, what would happen to art's questioning role, which has been one of its hallmarks in modernity? What type of social criticism can an ordinary urinal conduct in a Home Depot store or a can of Campbell soup at a Kroger's supermarket? Do we want a society where cans of soup are arranged *only* in the store or one where this type of display can *also* be used aesthetically for social commentary? If that is the case, we need to retain the ability to distinguish between the real and the imaginary cans. There has to be a time and place when a can of soup is not a can of soup but a commentary on commodification. We need, in other words, coun-terversions of nature, to examine the difference between a reality and its imagined reconstruction.

This is vital even in the realm of popular culture. When most major news organizations had accepted the Bush justification to invade Iraq, it was a fantasy news program, Jon Stewart's "The Daily Show," that leveled the sharpest volleys. The imaginary space allowed for art (of news that was not really news), allowed this program a critique the actual press had failed to conduct.[10] In short, even in the fluid world of commercial televi-sion, it is still vital for us to maintain some border between a verifiable reality and its satirized version.

But are the processes witnessed today leading to dedifferentiation, the return of art back to life? Of course, this question had already been posed by the avant-garde at the start of the twentieth century. Movements, like dada, undermined the definition of art by demonstrating the arbitrary link between art and nonart. If a bicycle wheel can be functional on the road but aesthetic in the museum, then what can art mean? But did this questioning result in the collapse of an autonomous art, as Gianni Vat-timo contends? By negating the sanctity of sites traditionally assigned to art, such as the concert hall, the gallery, the press, and by bringing art to the street, on the body, in the dump, the avant-garde weakened art's claim to separate status (1988: 53).

Vattimo's claim is no doubt true. But did the avant-garde strangle art as a distinct entity? Despite its nihilistic rhetoric to negate art, this movement constituted another step in aesthetic institutionalization, as Peter Bürger has shown (1984). This is also true for what Harold Rosenberg calls the "de-aestheticized art" of the 1960s and 1970s; it "has never been anything but an art movement" (1972).[11] In other words, while the avant-garde demonstrated that the line between art and nonart was arbitrary, it did not return the arts back to the street, a goal it had always claimed for itself. It simply expanded our definition of art.

Art still stands as a thing apart. Take for example Jeff Koons's monumental "Balloon Dog" (1994–2001), a pop art representation of a children's party favor.[12] Does this work crack the institution of art? Displayed in a gallery it functions as just as another sculpture, demanding the rigor of an aesthetic gaze. It may challenge our conception of art, but you cannot touch it or play with it. Is it ironic that children are not allowed to climb on it, run their fingers along its shiny surface, or slide down its back? This is what restoring art to life would suggest, that the difference between an art gallery and a playground would vanish. Do Vattimo and other theorists really believe this has taken place or that such crumbling of boundaries is even desirable?

They have understood autonomy too absolutely and too narrowly. If anything, the avant-garde further enhanced art's separation but with a twist—by showing that there was no essence in art.[13] If a hat rack stands in the exhibition space rather than the cloakroom of the gallery, then there could be nothing inherently artistic. In posing this subversive suggestion, readymade art revises the Platonic conflict between art and nature, provocatively disputing a one-to-one correspondence between truth and its representation. Does art replicate reality or reality replicate art? The claim that anything could become art does not mean that art is dead. For that hat rack acquires an aesthetic aura the moment it passes through the gallery, the boundary space of what I call the parabatic.

Of course, in aestheticizing mass-produced objects, the avant-garde succeeded in tarnishing art's luster. It not only cheapened the mystique of the original but it also exposed art's place in capitalism, as Benjamin pointed out through his theory of mechanical reproduction. But this commercialization of art began at roughly the time of art's differentiation, a century before the avant-garde.[14]

The excess of copies, of course, has led to the sullying of the aesthetic experience from an elitist perspective. When everyone can stick posters of Van Gogh's sunflowers on their walls, art forfeits the quasi-religious quality it once had in the palaces of aristocrats and kings. Yet, while art may have lost its preromantic aura, it has not been deprived of its monetary or cultural capital. Genuine art commands great prices at auction halls. All museums still prefer Greek sculpture to their Roman imitations (Gazda 2002). The real Mona Lisa and the original documents of the Magna Carta and the American Declaration of Independence possess almost talismanic energy, despite their availability in reproductions. The aesthetic aura still radiates.

Yet, critics are right. For about a hundred years aesthetic symbols have diffused throughout society by way of advertising, manufactured goods, canned music, the mass media, and more recently, the Internet. We can speak now of the general aestheticization of life where art bursts out of the galleries or musical halls to become a lifestyle. Like the body of Orpheus, the legendary musician, art is dismembered and scattered far and wide. Aesthetic images surround us at home, on the road, and in the workplace, as posters, billboards, and lights. Music now flows everywhere, from waiting rooms to elevators, to advertising, to iTunes, and to the World Wide Web—from reality to hyperreality.

Vattimo sees in this phenomenon the crumbling of aesthetic autonomy and the colonization of society by the aesthetic (2008: 56). By colonization Vattimo means a phenomenon first identified by Georg Simmel at the turn of the twentieth century, namely, the dissemination of aesthetic icons through every walk of life. The tragedy of modern culture, Simmel understood presciently, is that people feel overwhelmed in a sea of signs and ceaseless flux, "surrounded by an innumerable number of cultural elements" (1968: 44).

More recently other theorists have written on this relentless spread of consumer culture into every social nook. Under the pressures of post-Fordist capitalism, Jean Baudrillard has shown, culture has dissipated ubiquitously, no longer locatable in one place such as the university, the opera, or the gallery (1994: 149; 1981). Modern society, Terry Eagleton has argued, has been aestheticized, infiltrated by an aesthetic ideology that fosters a "non-coercive consensus" (1990: 97). According to Fredric

Jameson, everything in society, "from economic values and state power to practices and the very structure of the psyche can be said to have become 'cultural'" (Jameson 1984: 87).[15] Likewise, the French sociologist, Michel Maffesoli believes that the aesthetic has become a shared sentiment binding us together. People in Western societies, he argues, form associations of lifestyle and affective attraction. Rather than suffering from isolation, modern individuals are connected by common ways of feeling and experiencing (1996: 81).

It is hard to know specifically what aestheticization means for these writers. Are political decisions deferred to or melted in an aesthetic realm? Do we find in the aesthetic an imaginary reconciliation of life's problems? The process implies that art breaks out of its confines, diffuses through society, and exercises its authority over it. Like Midas, it turns everything into glittering ornament, baubles of our desires. While the radiance of high art may be fading, the aesthetic, according to these theories, has an afterglow, illuminating all parts of life.

Is there a touch of aestheticism in these descriptions? Whereas aestheticism in the nineteenth century idealized art, celebrating its capacity to shape life, today this concept grants the aesthetic extraordinary powers to affect social relations. For the aesthetic has acquired enormous force to bind us through imperceptible webs of feelings, impressions, and sensations, bringing about a social consensus. If this indeed has taken place, then art has extended its influence beyond its dominion, committing a disciplinary hubris that Plato himself could hardly have imagined.

But is this a subjugation of society or more simply a crossover of boundaries? What we may be witnessing is the continued interpenetration of the aesthetic, economic, and political realms rather than the colonization of society by culture. Even this overlap of borders does not really announce the disintegration of autonomy. We still continue to make aesthetic judgments and posit divisions between forms of aesthetic practice. While we may ignore a tune in the dentist's office, we appreciate it when we listen to it on an iPod. A fan of hip-hop, for instance, would never confuse a concert with a political rally or a religious ceremony even though she might see certain features shared by all three occasions.

By the same token, a painting, a CD of popular music, or a video does not have the same cultural value as a key chain, a toothbrush, or a seashell. To be sure, Andy Warhol's depictions of Campbell soup are not stored in the supermarket, and they certainly have more monetary worth than the ones in our kitchens. Why? Because of the aesthetic aura, because we still divide aesthetic objects from ordinary ones even if these divisions are never permanent. We also discriminate among various forms of aesthetic experience, be this viewing a mountain vista, reading a poem, looking at a face, watching a gymnastics performance, or listening to music. The collapse of autonomy would mean the loss of perceptible markers between art and nonart—a state of being that has not existed since the time of Euripides.

Indeed, Athenians strolling around the Acropolis of the fifth century would have confronted a dizzying array of aesthetic objects, sites, and sounds—from tombstone reliefs, to oratory, to theater. There was art everywhere, a fact recognized by Pericles when he honored his city's "love of what is beautiful." In short, the Athenians experienced a saturation of the arts before their compartmentalization, a situation aspired to by the critics of autonomy. But the Athenians made distinctions between poetry and nonpoetry, a theatrical performance and a political tract, a beautiful amphora and an ugly one. Although they would have understood a speech by Demosthenes and a tragedy by Sophocles as performative, they would never have confused one for the other.

An Organic Art?

Critics of aesthetic autonomy often ignore this point. They presume that art's disintegration and scattering would lead us to some predifferentiated state when art was one object among other objects. In this, they are the heirs of Johann Joachim Winckelmann (1717–68), the German founder of art history and hagiographer of Greek society. He believed that the Greeks had an unmediated relationship to nature, whereas we are removed from it; they imitated nature, whereas we can only copy the Greeks ([1755] 1987: 33).[16] For him antiquity was something to be polished and reproduced and no longer to be built on.

The critics of today, of course, share neither Winckelmann's idealization of Greek society nor his unproblematic association of Greek art with nature. But there is a residual organicism in their conception of art's integrity before its differentiation. When they celebrate the historical avant-garde as art's return to its social niche or when they glorify the postmodern explosion of culture into a myriad elements scattered throughout society, they tacitly align themselves to an intellectual tradition that deified Greek art as original and natural. They regard the avant-garde and postmodernism as examples of "de-differentiation," as attempts to return to a time before the slide of alienation, to a time of naïve rather than sentimental art.

I am referring here to Friedrich Schiller's (1759–1805) distinction between naïve and sentimental poetry. The naïve poet, according to Schiller, is tied effortlessly to nature, embraces spontaneity, and has little self-awareness. The sentimental poet, on the other hand, thinks critically and intellectually, feels alienated from life, and distrusts unmediated inspiration and feelings. To the naïve poet "nature must be victorious over art" ([1795] 1966: 89), by which Schiller meant that nature subsumes art making. The naïve person "overlooks" the artificial, has no time for criticism (i.e., theory), and is dependent on experience (92, 154). Because the Greeks were familiar with nature, one finds so little "sentimental interest" among them. This is why, according to Friedrich Schlegel (1772–1829), the "interesting" remains the standard of aesthetic worth. But Homer was "never" interesting to his contemporaneous listeners, because they found in him magic, force, poetry, and wisdom (2001: 83). The sentimental poet, by contrast, can be only satirical or elegiac, pondering the contradictions between actuality and the unattainability of perfection (Schiller 1966: 117).

Although the critics of aesthetic autonomy lack Schiller's romanticized vocabulary, they too long for a time when art was just a thing, when opera was street theater, music was background noise, painting was body art, and sculpture served totemic worship. Yet even Schiller himself realized that such a return was impossible. He detected impulses of poetic self-consciousness and social differentiation by the fourth century BCE, recognizing a perceptible difference between the poetics of Euripides and Aeschylus, for instance ([1795] 1966: 104). Schiller moreover could identify no naïve poets in Latin and only Shakespeare in the Renaissance.

Today we are still dealing with the consequences of Schiller's proposal—that we can only have sentimental art, an art that, as Hegel understood, achieved "self-transcendence . . . but within its own sphere and in the form of art itself" (1975: 80). The critique of aesthetic autonomy is really a critique of this differentiated art. Not a spontaneous creation of nature or of inspired artists, autonomous art regards itself as manufactured. Above all, it thinks about its constructed nature, drawing attention to itself as artificial, and in this way, highlighting the difference between the natural and the synthetic, between the real and the invented. In so doing, it performs a useful social function.

Autonomy then seems the only possible state for art today, characterized by self-reflection and distance. A glimmer of this comes out in the conversations Stephen Dedalus has with his friends in Joyce's *A Portrait of the Artist as a Young Man*. Stephen's conception of art is rather straightforward.[17] Art, he tells Lynch, is the "human disposition of sensible or intelligible matter for an esthetic end" ([1916] 1976). How does it accomplish this? It expresses and presses "from the gross earth" or "from the prison gates of our soul" an image of beauty (206). But the artist needs a distance both from this earth and his soul, as Stephen himself knows when he declares his independence from the "nets" of nationality, language, and religion (203). When at the end of the novel Stephen announces to Cranly that he cannot serve what he can no longer believe in (home, fatherland, church) he says famously that he would express himself in his art with "silence, exile, and cunning" (247). In essence, you have to leave home in order to write about it. Joyce could portray Dublin only from the remove of Trieste and Paris. "Isolation is the first principle of artistic economy," says Stephen in *Stephen Hero* (1977: 34).

Stephen's sense of detachment is another way of characterizing the portal separating fantasy and reality that I am dealing with here. This gateway signals literature's parabatic capacity to mediate between the actual Dublin and its representation in Joyce's *Dubliners* and *Ulysses*. Rather than leading to some authentic place, literature features the tension between artifice and verisimilitude. In so doing, it reminds readers that knowing the world is a matter of interacting with truth and fiction.

§3 Of Two Autonomies

"Ernst ist das Leben, heiter ist die Kunst"
—Friedrich Schiller, *Wallenstein*[1]

If art has always danced with truth, alternatively embracing or snubbing it, this performance has stumbled in modernity. With art turning into itself and going its own way, philosophers and poets legitimately asked if art wanted to be true to reality or to itself. Do we discover the world through art or are we entrapped in its world, by definition a lie? Schiller's terse characterization above captures our dilemma. Art's frivolity compares badly to life's earnestness.

I have argued that we have rejected art because of its self-conscious interiority, its celebration of form, and its apparent indifference to injustice. We have condemned it, in other words, because of its autonomy. Here I would like to disentangle the arguments and propose that we have misunderstood the idea of aesthetic autonomy. For instead of one, there are two autonomies, one social and the other ideological. The first has to do with the gradual rise of art as a separate space of human activity, a new way of organizing, disseminating, and consuming the arts. The other posits art as the basis for social relations.

When philosophers in the eighteenth century began thinking about the distinctive principles of beauty, they were expressing conceptually a development that was taking place in society to which they had contributed but over which they had little control—the social compartmentalization of art that occurred in tandem with the specialization of other social domains. They were actually coming to terms with the vocational differentiation of social life. For instance, Moses Mendelsohn (1729–86) and his pupil, Karl Philipp Moritz (1756–93), were the first to classify the various arts into one category. Gotthold Ephraim Lessing (1729–81) attempted in his treatise, *Laocoön* ([1766] 1965), to distinguish poetry from the plastic arts.[2] These thinkers were grouping the arts together under the name of aesthetic autonomy. Just as important, they were conceiving works of art as objects of the viewer's/reader's contemplation/interpretation.[3]

Kant's Aesthetics

The trouble began with the way these philosophers justified the assessment of a beautiful object. Immanuel Kant (1724–1804), for instance, contended—with reference to natural rather than artistic beauty—that the observer has a disinterested relationship to that object in so far as she has no other intention with respect to the object than the pleasurable apprehension of its formal properties. Kant described this process with his notoriously paradoxical phrase "*Zweckmäsigkeit ohne Zweck*," usually translated as purposiveness without a purpose: "*Beauty* is the form of the *purposiveness* of an object, so far as this is perceived in it *without any representation of a purpose*" (Kant [1790] 2000: 90). The aesthetic judgment, which determines whether something is beautiful or not, aspires to a goal without ever reaching it, having no cognitive or practical function, such as to gain knowledge or find nourishment, apart from appreciation of the formal features in the object. Form, in other words, is a destination in itself.

In claiming that the judgment of taste could not be reduced to a concept, Kant recognized the special aspect of the aesthetic, namely, that it could not be transposed to the world of knowable things. Beauty cannot be contained or described because it is inexhaustible. "If we judge Objects merely according to concepts, then all representation of beauty is lost. Thus there can be no rule according to which anyone is forced to recognize anything as beautiful." (62). Aesthetic perception does not function in a cognitive manner and agreement in matters of beauty cannot be reached through conceptual exercises. In short, no single description can ever capture or possess a beautiful object because the world of the senses and feelings operates differently from the world of knowing.

When Kant proposed that the aesthetic judgment was not reducible to reason, he was reworking soil already tilled by Alexander Gottlieb Baumgarten (1714–62) who in his groundbreaking, *Reflections on Poetry* (1735), identified the aesthetic as a separate category. By distinguishing between the *noeta* (things known) from the *aestheta* (things perceived), Baumgarten argued that the former fell within the faculty of logic whereas the latter fell within the faculty of perception or the "aesthetic" (1954: 116). Kant appropriated the distinctiveness of the aesthetic and then ennobled it with universality through the concept of disinterestedness. For unlike taste, which for Kant was subjective, the aesthetic judgment had inter-subjective validity because it was disinterested and pure.[4]

Kant ascribed to beauty one particular quality, an inner organization, which triggered in the observer the free play of imagination and understanding [sec 217]. Beauty then is not subordinated to reason but comes to be in this accord of imagination with understanding. Beauty thus lies less in the formal qualities of the object than in the mental facilities of a person, what earlier theorists understood as the faculty of taste (the human property preoccupied with beauty). For Kant, then, the consideration of beauty is a judgment on the part of the freethinking individual, and beauty exists to the extent that it stirs pleasure in the beholder. It comes into being as an interaction between object and subject (Esser 1995: 14). Despite the way later thinkers and artists have interpreted Kant, he never claimed that beauty stands as an absolute value in an ethereal space. It is, above all, a relational entity.

Nevertheless, his position implies that both observer and object are located in a valueless sphere, free from social, economic, religious, and political compulsions. It is based on a conception of the person as a self-reflecting and self-determining individual rather than as a social being, subject to social laws and implicated in economic and political relations. Many poststructuralist thinkers trace to this stance the root of aestheticism.

These critics, however, have neglected the radical nature of Kant's argument and the fact that we are beholden to it in our conception of intellectual freedom. By claiming that taste is disinterested, Kant distinguished aesthetic from other modes of judgment. He freed, in other words, the aesthetic experience from utility, morality, and science, a move that paralleled the gradual institutionalization of art. "The interest in the *Beautiful of Art* . . . furnishes no proof whatever of a disposition attached to the morally good" (2000: 177). From this point on, people could call an object beautiful without worrying whether it was good or useful, a momentous step mostly lost in the current debunking of aesthetic autonomy.

We feel the impact of this development in our visceral belief that the artist and intellectual should be independent of state regulation. Specifically, we can see Kant's contribution in his effort to secure intellectual freedom for the philosopher and for the university in general. Although German Enlightenment scholars did not have to face the violence of the Inquisition, like Galileo, they had to confront the power of doctrinaire theologians and, more important, the censorship of the Prussian state, especially after the death of Frederick the Great and the succession of his religiously conservative nephew, Frederick William II. After the publication of *Religion within the Limits of Mere Reason* (1793), Kant was officially reprimanded by Frederick William II for misrepresenting Christianity and threatened with punitive measures (Chaouli 2003: 60). Kant reproduced this remonstrance in the preface to *The Conflict of the Faculties* (1798) in which he described his mistreatment by the king and his minister of justice. Interestingly, Kant made recourse to the narrowness of disciplinary specialization, pointing out that his volume was an "unintelligible, closed book, only a debate among scholars" rather than a matter of public debate (1979: 15).

Kant expanded this argument in *The Conflict of the Faculties* where he argued that some members of the university should be free from state authority. Although accepting government regulation in practical disciplines, like theology, law, and medicine, he supported scholarly freedom in the faculty of philosophy (i.e., the humanities, social and natural sciences) because it was for Kant propelled by reason to examine truth. The power "to judge autonomously," he asserted, is reason. "So the philosophy faculty, because it must answer for the truth of the teachings it is to adopt . . . must be conceived as free and subject only to laws of reason, not by the government" (1979: 43). Humanists could speculate about the nature of the world in the way that theologians, doctors, and lawyers could not about God, medicine, and justice. In taking this position, Kant reinforced the critical dimension of humanistic enquiry against an unbending theology and a steely state.

Kant's struggle to gain greater independence for intellectuals from autocratic rulers should be seen as part of a greater effort to carve out a sovereign space for art, which Ferenc Feher characterizes as a "self-liberation." The principal "battle fought for autonomy of the aesthetic sphere was that between religion, on the one hand, and art and literature, on the other" (1986: 37–38). In the stratified societies of pre-Enlightenment Europe, artists were, in a sense, servants, dependent on the wealth and prestige of aristocratic or church patrons (Schulte-Sasse 1989: 87). These patrons often made exact demands for the works they commissioned. Leonardo

Da Vinci, for instance, signed a contract for his "Virgin of the Rocks" that specified the content, the color of the Virgin's robe, date of delivery, and guarantee of future repairs (Shiner 2001: 6).

Contemporary critics of the aesthetic often ignore this historical situation and the link philosophers had made between intellectual and aesthetic sovereignty. It was as epistemologically essential to liberate the scholar from the theologian and censor as it was to distinguish the beautiful from the good and the moral, to see art not just a reflection of reality, a symbol in a religious rite, a stepping stone to the ethical life, but as a world unto itself.

In proposing his idea of autonomy and the universality of the judgment of taste, Kant sought to avoid both an ontological conception of beauty (a thing as inherently beautiful) and a subjective one (beauty existing in the eye of the beholder). He located the judgments of taste in the human response to beauty, in a faculty common to all. At the same time, he proposed the perception of beauty as a collective experience, a matter of discussion. We all agree in matters of taste because we share an apprehension of beauty that gives judgments of taste universal validity rather than because objects are inherently beautiful. Even though Kant attempted to escape the subjectivism of British theorists, like Hume, by placing questions of taste in a universal sphere, he too sought the aesthetic in the responses of the individual rather than in the object itself (Jay 2003: 6–7).[5] Taste then is a kind of common sense. When we judge an object, we compare "our judgment with the possible rather than the actual judgments of others, and by putting ourselves in the place of any other man, by abstracting from the limitations which contingently attach to our own judgment" (Kant 2000: 170).

Kant's idea of universality here presumes an individual seeking agreement with others on matters of beauty. Critics who equate Kant with aestheticism or who see the aesthetic as a free-floating concept, overlook the social rootedness of his thinking. His idea of consensus implies that aesthetic evaluation is part of a collective process. A man abandoned on a desert island, Kant noted, would not seek to adorn himself. "The Beautiful interests only in *society*." This is so because of humanity's natural propensity to "sociability," that is, our drive to "communicate our *feelings*" to others (2000: 174). People, in other words, tacitly acknowledge the social dimension of art when they expect others to respond to their aesthetic evaluations.

Art then is communal practice or even a "political activity," as Hannah Arendt put it. What binds art and politics is that "they are both phenomena of the public world" (1977: 218).[6] The capacity to judge requires that people see things not only from their own perspective but also from that of others in the public realm. Kant located this practice in the phenomenon of taste, which, although previously considered a private matter, he opened to public discussion. "Culture and politics, then, belong together because it is not knowledge or truth which is at stake, but rather judgment and decision, the judicious exchange of opinion about the sphere of public life and the common world" (Arendt 223).

Aesthetic judgment then is a dialogical process, more socially constrained than its detractors believe.[7] "The aesthetic moment in Kant replicates rather than resolves the tensions between the individual and community" so central to the position of the subject in the world (Cascardi 1991: 12). What this suggests is that judgments of taste presuppose controversy. They are made with reference to a community that expects some agreement. If these conditions do not apply, "we would not be able so much as to quarrel about them, or they would not be of the kind we call aesthetic" (20). We squabble about them because, as Ted Cohen explains, "to take something to be art is to suppose that it matters" to us how other people understand art (1988: 11).

Art exists as a process of social exchange. A beautiful object, Alexander Nehamas explains, induces in us a longing "to go beyond what is standing before us" (2000: 402). Not only do we want to make it part of our life, we want to talk to other people about this experience. This interaction with others, makes the desire for beauty an essentially social phenomenon; "it needs to be communicated to others and pursued in their company" (2007: 77).

We get a sense of this reciprocity in Thomas Mann's novella, *Death in Venice*. As the artist Gustave Aschenbach realizes his attraction to Tadzio, at the beginning he feels "a father's kindness toward him: such an emotion as the possessor of beauty can inspire in one who has offered himself up in spirit to create beauty" (1986: 35). Stirred by the boy's radiance, Aschenbach finds a new motivation in the last few weeks of his life on the beach of Venice during an outbreak of cholera. Tadzio himself picks up the older man's attraction, offering him furtive smiles in exchange for his interest.

We cede something to the work in front of us, allowing it to affect us as we in turn appraise it. But this very procedure of evaluation is public.

The work compels us "to expose private feelings to the judgment of other people while at the same time imagining them as members of an affective community that shares common goals and objects" (Siebers 1998: 46–47). This assessment is without social import if made on an isolated island. It is irrelevant in the same way Marcel Mauss says that a free gift is impossible. The act of giving immediately places the receiver in a position of compulsion. The present makes sense in a ritual of "obligations of exchange and contract" ([1923–24] 1990: 5). Mauss's depiction of the "system of the gift" as "disinterested and obligatory" (33) captures the paradoxical nature of aesthetic valuation, being public and private at the same time.

We can admire a sunset, or a child's face, the motion of an athlete, or the rhythm of a poem without gaining anything from the experience apart from aesthetic pleasure. Or as Elaine Scarry put it, "people seem to wish there to be beauty even when their own self-interest is not served" (1999: 123). This is what Kant meant with the idea of disinterestedness. Once we engage with other people about our aesthetic experience, however, this experience enters the social realm.

Art as Social Space

This private/public duality is reflected in the historical rise of art. The Kantian isolation of the aesthetic occurred in tandem with the social differentiation of art in the eighteenth and nineteenth centuries. Rather than imposing the concept of aesthetic autonomy on reality, philosophers witnessed and helped promote this institutionalization. Both developments, philosophical and social, occurred simultaneously, mutually reinforcing each other.

It is important to make this distinction because the attack on aesthetic autonomy and the consequent rejection of art twists these two strands of autonomy into one. It identifies aestheticism with a broader phenomenon of differentiation while failing to recognize sufficiently the cultural and epistemological implication of art's compartmentalization.

Art's newly acquired materiality, for instance, manifested itself in the organization of aristocratic art collections. While works of art were once placed indiscriminately alongside special objects such as rocks, feathers, seashells, coins, and stuffed animals, in the eighteenth century they were separated into a more prized and specialized assortment (Sheehan 2000: 19). In time, these collections included painting and sculpture exclusively as examples of fine art, bringing together disparate periods and societies into one historical sweep and open to public view.[8] Concurrently concert halls and theaters, formerly housed within palaces, were built for general audiences. The great national museums, theaters, and music halls of Europe literally moved out of aristocratic houses.

In similar vein, literature, now having incorporated poetry, the novel, drama, and satire, too acquired the attributes of an institution—the publishing house, the school, the press, the literary agency, the magazine, café, reading society, and book club. The relative autonomy of literature came to be characterized "by specific formal and organizational properties" and maintained by boundaries that interact with other activities in separate domains (Bennett 1990: 127).[9]

In short, there appeared in the eighteenth century the philosophical discourse on the aesthetic and the social system of the arts, two interrelated phenomena. We have to disentangle the two, however—the social compartmentalization of art from the talk about art—in order to address the charge of aestheticism leveled against art. Aestheticism, alternatively labeled aesthetic ideology, promulgates the view that art governs social life.[10]

Aesthetic Autonomy Is not Art for Art's Sake

Although Kant never espoused this position, seeing beauty as a relational concept, his work contributed to the rise of a belief that art existed as a *Ding-an-sich*, self-sufficient, self-contained, and self-referential. In its most radical permutation, this ideology accorded primacy to aesthetic dimensions in human consciousness (Chytry 1989: xii), promoting an historical weltanschauung, which saw society and the state as works of art or built on an aesthetic base.

The penchant to aestheticize social life inspired many thinkers, not least Schiller. A strong supporter of the French Revolution, he grew disenchanted with its violent turn and sought in art the basis for politics. His sublimation of politics, however, was a far cry from Pericles' tribute to the Athenian love of beauty and freedom or even from Winckelmann's belief in the correlation of art and political freedom in Greece.[11] Schiller placed his faith in the power of the aesthetic to transform society. We can only approach the problem of politics through the aesthetic, he laid out, freedom being attainable only through beauty ([1795] 1967: 9). Schiller elevated political freedom as a great virtue, even as he reduced politics to art by contending that everyone is a free citizen in the aesthetic state (219).

Schiller prepared the groundwork for the eventual construction of an aesthetic interpretation of life. In so doing, he imposed a great burden on the aesthetic to the extent that he saw in it the power to suspend the negative consequences of modernization, such as social alienation, environmental degradation, and ruthless economic competition. Civilization (Kultur), he argued, inflicted a wound on humanity through increase in knowledge, the divisions in the world of letters (*Scheidung der Wissenchaften*), and the "increasing complex machinery of State" that necessitated a more rigorous separation of ranks and occupations (32–33). In this world of unceasing specialization "only the aesthetic mode of communication unites society" (215). Schiller saw this social partitioning as a breakup of social life, which he found particularly harmful in comparison to the perceived unity of classical society. There was a paradox in his reaction, however. While he bewailed the dangers of social differentiation, he believed (autonomous) art facilitated communication among social domains, thereby overcoming social fragmentariness.

Through the work of Schiller and other writers the aesthetic emerged in the second half of the eighteenth century as a space of redemption suspending the consequences of social compartmentalization (Schulte-Sasse, 1989: 87). Many thinkers, in other words, saw in the aesthetic an answer to the wider vocational specialization around them. Facing the disenchantment of the world, described decades later by Max Weber,[12] German Romantics came increasingly to see art as an oasis in a society sacrificing all values to calculation, losing traditional work to specialization, and surrendering magic to intellectualization.

The Ambivalence of Autonomy

Many critics use Schiller's claim as a bludgeon against the idea of aesthetic autonomy. They argue that this view compensates for art's powerlessness by endowing it with special faculties to relieve the pain of modernity. Art obviously could never perform this palliative task. But why must we take Schiller's arguments, or Oscar Wilde's for that matter, as valid explanations of art's social role? These writers contradicted themselves in their daily practice.

While Enlightenment intellectuals were praising the purity of the aesthetic, they were also converting the arts, particularly literature, into the grand project of social engineering through schooling. That they adopted such a Horatian understanding of aesthetic value undermines the very idea of art as a haven of redemption. Perhaps nothing undercuts the view that art exists autonomously in bourgeois society more "than the fact that it is precisely in such a society that works of art have been made educational instruments in the socialization process both inside and outside of schools" (Bürger 1985/86: 15).

Enlightenment intellectuals aimed, to borrow from Schiller's title, at the aesthetic education of man. The figure that best exemplifies this connection between aesthetics and politics is Wilhelm von Humboldt (1767–1835), a close friend of Goethe and Schiller. The author of numerous studies ranging from philology, linguistics, to aesthetics, and political philosophy, he served briefly as Prussian minister of education during which time he established the University of Berlin. This university, in a sense, institutionalized the sovereign structure that Kant had envisioned for the faculty of philosophy, endowing it with some independence vis-à-vis state regulation while conscripting it in the service of the public good.

The Enlightenment also witnessed art's entry into the market. As artists gained freedom from the representational culture of the court, they sought to make a living in the competitive world of capitalism. Literary authors, for instance, having to struggle with popular writers to gain a readership that had been previously ensured by the aristocracy, came to see themselves as "producers of goods" (Fontius 1977: 498). They had no choice but to sell their work like other producers.

Changing market conditions in the seventeenth and eighteenth centuries undermined the one-to-one relationships of patronage and enforced specialization on everyone, including artists. Indeed, they had to recognize that the market now established literary worth by separating the successful from the unsuccessful. Given this ruthless reality, it is understandable that artists (and philosophers) acted defensively at the loss of ecclesiastical and aristocratic patronage and at the capacity of the anonymous market to determine aesthetic value. In short, aesthetic ideology emerged, not coincidently, alongside two overwhelming developments: the commodification of art and its incorporation within the modern curriculum.[13]

Artists came to realize that art could not exist outside of the world of published books, salons, and music halls, even though many were claiming the opposite in their writings. Just because these artists (and critics) represented themselves as internal exiles and their work as immaculately pure, does not mean that either was untouched by market forces. Indeed, literary texts themselves tackled this paradox, the tension between the desire for independence and the pull of money and fame.

Balzac's *Lost Illusions* (1842), for instance, dramatizes this conflict while validating the autonomy for art. Written between 1837 and 1843, the novel is set at the turn of the nineteenth century, before "the Stanhope press and the ink-distributing roller" had arrived into the provinces. David Séchard, the printer in the town of Angouleme, senses that the time of mass production has come. "There will be a demand for cheap clothes and cheap books, just as pictures today are small because no one now has the space for large ones." Knowing that these new products would not last, he works on inventing a new type of paper against this obsolescence. "So the problem to be solved is of the greatest importance to literature, to science,—and to economics" (1997: 110). David could never have predicted that these new processes of mass production that were to save literature would also subjugate it to the cruel laws of commerce.

This is confirmed by the tragic experience of his close friend and brother-in-law, Lucien Chardon, who goes to Paris in search of poetic fame. Incapable of surviving, let alone triumphing as an artist, in the heartless world of the capital, Lucien is forced to become a journalist, a hack, seeking publicity. "For artists, the great problem is to attract notice," Lucien is told before arriving in Paris (143). This astute observation on the necessity of making a "buzz" is a direct product of a print-based society, as Elizabeth Eisenstein, has confirmed. The anxiety "about getting attention and holding it was . . . built into the trade of the new professional author." The author's meager rewards and prestige depended on "printed publicity—like those of any business firm" (1979: 156).

The writer builds his reputation by hawking his products. Lucien gets a sense of this crass commercialism when he overhears a conversation between a bookseller and a publisher: "Would you take five hundred copies? If you do I will let you have them at five francs, and give you fourteen to the dozen" (Balzac 1997: 203). This dialogue, as if about croissants, begins gradually to introduce the "provincial celebrity" to the crudeness and harshness of the book world in Paris. The publisher Dauriat confirms this when he tells Lucien that "I do not find it amusing to risk two thousand francs on publishing a book in the hope of making two thousand:

I speculate in literature" (279). In Dauriat's world there is no place for poetry. If anyone comes in with a manuscript of poetry, he says curtly, show him the door. He had lost too much money on poetry the year before.

Even with Dauriat's exaggerated language, it is hard not to miss the irony here. David's ambition to develop cheap paper to support Lucien in Paris and his wife at home were contributing to the "destruction" of literature. "And so, by a strange coincidence, while Lucien was caught up in the machinery of journalism, where he seemed likely to leave his honor and his intelligence torn to shreds in its vast mechanism, David Séchard, at the back of his printing house, was confronting the material aspect of the phenomenon of newspapers and periodicals" (500). It is difficult not to get disillusioned, Lucien concludes, when "everything is for sale, and everything is manufactured, even success" (396).

Balzac's novel highlights the tug-of-war between the belief in the social independence of art and the reality of its social embeddedness. In a sense, the novel itself manifested this conflict, putting into doubt the ahistorical claims about literature's ideological liberation from its environment. By referring to the role of critics, reviewers, editors, publishers, sellers, and buyers in Paris, Balzac was at the same time pointing to the institutionalization of literature, its very autonomy. That is to say, Balzac himself understood that this autonomy was paradoxically a public process by which literature became a social domain in its own right, taking shape in the places that Lucien visits—the newspaper, the publishing house, the editor's office, the coffeehouse. Or rather, we can argue that this process was made possible by the changes in society that authors so decried—specialization, professionalization, capitalism, and the growth of state bureaucracy. Aesthetic autonomy then expresses nothing else but these very social forces that created art as a distinct sphere. It manifests art's double character—that it is both free and chained at the same time.

Art's dual nature comes into the fore in George Gissing's Victorian novel, *New Grub Street* (1891). Like Balzac's work, it expresses the artist's disenchantment with the commercialization of fiction. Many of Gissing's characters, like Edwin Reardon, the protagonist and a novelist, are resentful because they are undermined by the commercial enterprise they are forced to work in. At the onset of the novel, Jasper Milvain, a journalist, remarks over breakfast that Reardon "isn't the kind of man to keep up literary production as a paying business" (36).[14] Nowadays, he complains, literature has become a "trade" and "your successful man of letters is a tradesman" (38). Marian Yule, the daughter of the disillusioned critic, Alfred Yule, reiterates this dark judgment. Toiling away in the reading room of the British Museum, she asks why she should exhaust herself "in the manufacture of printed stuff which no one even pretended to be more than a commodity for the day's market. What unspeakable folly!" (137) She wonders whether someone could invent a "literary machine" into which one could throw old books "and have them reduced, blended, modernized into a single one for today's consumption" (138).[15] The hyperbolic metaphor of literature as another cog in the industrial mechanism nevertheless presents a sobering picture of fiction as book production. This is automatic writing before hypertext.

Is it a coincidence that this novel, so searing in its exploration of literature's underside, was published the same year as Oscar Wilde's *The Picture of Dorian Gray*, and seven years after Huysmans' *À Rebours*, both ostentatious examples of European aestheticism? Gissing's work condemned what Art for Art's Sake thought it had evaded, the commoditization of art. But artists decried this phenomenon while they participated in it. Of course, some may argue that artists embraced the idea of aesthetic autonomy to elude ideologically the realities of the market in a profitless, disinterested realm.[16] Whatever their motivations, they subscribed to an understanding of art as a public phenomenon even while they celebrated the notion of pure form. They did so not only in the promotion of their own work—the necessity of finding publishers, doing readings, sending the book to reviewers—but also in their engagement with the productions of popular culture—incorporating material from detective fiction, magazines, and advertising.

Autonomous Art Is Public Art

This contradiction perhaps is best played out in modernism, which, like the Art for Art's Sake that preceded it, deified spotless form. In a typical argument, the painter, Kasimir Malevich (1878–1935), wrote in his essay on suprematism, that the general public must become accustomed to nonobjective art. "Art no longer cares to serve the state and religion, it no longer wishes to illustrate the history of manners, it wants to have nothing further to do with the object, as such, and believes that it can exist, in and for itself, without 'things'" ([1927] 1964: 95). Malevich's pronouncement manifests modernism's take-no-prisoners attitude with respect to the audience. But could this theory ever come to describe art, even modernist art at that? Could art really exist "in and for itself"?

Oscar Wilde, the high priest of European aestheticism, doubted this. He understood the indispensable function of the audience in the complex operations of the art world.[17] "Diversity of opinion about a work of art," he wrote in the Preface to *The Picture of Dorian Gray*, "shows that the work is new, complex, and vital" ([1890] 1974: xxxiii). It is the audience, Wilde says, that validates the work's efficacy and is the ultimate object of its defamiliarizing strategies and of the artist's social criticism.[18]

Constantine Cavafy (1863–1933), steeped in English and French aestheticism, keenly appreciated the crucial role the reader played in the public game of art. On the one hand, Cavafy, the modernist, saw art as an elitist act, produced by artists for a small coterie of readers. "Of the Shop" shows how an artisan puts up for sale his second-rate works, preferring to keep his true "artistic" creations for himself. His finest creations are those he "judges, / wants, and regards as beautiful; / not as he observed or studied them in nature." Rather than selling them, he locks away these examples of his "daring work" (Cavafy 1963: 50).[19] The language of the poem, bare, unmetaphorical, prosaic, befits the unyielding approach the text itself espouses toward the audience.

But could Cavafy sustain this aestheticist view? In practice he understood that art was a public phenomenon, involving many intermediaries. Unlike the aloof artist of the poem, Cavafy was energetically involved in the distribution and public reception of his work. Like few other poets, he attempted to influence the public consumption of his poetry by refusing to publish a collected edition of his work (Jusdanis 1987). He chose, instead, to have poems circulate in folders or chapbooks that he could recall, to revise or rearrange. In his poetry Cavafy glorified form and elevated art as the supreme human value. But in daily life, he considered poetry and art collective activities, requiring the ultimate notarization of the audience.

The need for public confirmation of aesthetic status comes out in another modernist text, "The Beldonald Holbein," by Henry James. Notorious for his elliptical dialogue, refracted representations, and intense character analysis, James offers an unexpected social portrayal of art. The narrator, an artist, has been actively seeking to paint the portrait of Mrs. Brash, the companion of the wealthy American expatriate in England, Lady Beldonald, seeing in her a modern Holbein figure. Insulted that he

would choose the plain Mrs. Brash, over her, Lady Beldonald surrepti-
tiously engineers the repatriation of her companion to "a minor American city." Having just discovered her disappearance, the narrator and his
friend, Mrs. Munden, compare the unlucky Mrs. Brash to a painting
gone out of style:

> It wasn't—the minor American city—a market for Holbeins, and what had
> occurred was that the poor old creature, banished from its museum and
> refreshed by the rise of no new movement to hand it, was capable of the
> miracle of a silent revolution, of itself turning, in its dire dishonor, its face to
> the wall. So it stood, without the intervention of a ghost of a critic, till they
> happened to pull it round again and find it mere paint." (1903: 48)

Without the "intervention" of buyers, visitors, and critics, the painting
could not become art at all, having been reduced to colors on a canvass—
a potential art work, much like the trinkets in Cavafy's poem, rather
than a social construct.

Insofar as artists publish, exhibit, or sell their work, they tacitly accept
the communal and communicative character of art, even if they end up
rejecting the very community that validates their oeuvre.[20] It goes without
saying that artists produce their work according to aesthetic norms that
they either violate or abide with. A work of art, Jan Mukarovsky explains,
"oscillates between the past and future status of an aesthetic norm" that is
established in the social sphere (1970: 36). All works of art, then "possess
extra-aesthetic value" (88), even those claiming to be pure form.

Modernist poets accepted art as a constructed category, despite their
aestheticist stances. Contrary to a dominant position represented by Andreas Huyssen in *After the Great Divide*, the characterization of modernism as socially aloof does not hold up under closer examination. The
central push of Huyssen's thesis is that "modernism constituted itself
through a conscious strategy of exclusion, an anxiety of contamination
by its other: an increasingly consuming and engulfing mass culture"
(1986: vii). This is what he calls "the Great Divide," a discourse which
"insists on the categorical distinction between high art and mass culture"
and which reigned between 1880 and 1920.

Huyssen's position represents a misreading of modernism, taking modernist theories and manifestoes at face value. It accepts, in other words,
modernism's apparent rejection of popular culture and its differentiation
of mass from real art. Not all critics share this position. Decades be-

fore poststructuralism, Walter Benjamin discovered that Mallarmé, the prophet of pure form, had appropriated tropes from the mass media. "Un coup de dès," for instance, has long been hailed as one of the most uncompromising reflections on the distilled meaning of words. Yet, Mallarmé was in this work "the first to incorporate the graphic tensions of the advertisement in the printed page" (Benjamin 1978: 77). Earlier than most poets, Mallarmé also foresaw and assimilated the features of cinema in his work, as I show in the last chapter.[21]

More recently, critics have uncovered similar parallels between high modernism and popular culture. Mark S. Morrisson has demonstrated that the modernists' engagements with the commercial mass market were "rich and diverse." He argues that these authors were "savvy about promotion and the audience" and modernist texts, like the "Nausicaa" chapter in *Ulysses*, contained the words, images, and slogans found in magazines (2001: 5–6).

Even self-conscious snobs like T. S. Eliot, so ostentatiously hostile to mass movements, had a working relationship with them. A reexamination of his oeuvre reveals "the constant presence of popular culture in his creative process" (Chinitz 1995: 240). Rather than seeing high and popular art as dichotomous, Eliot traced a continuous line between the two. His readings in anthropology taught him that the arts were functionally differentiated but part of social practice (238).

American modernism likewise engaged actively with mass culture. Faced with a crisis of value in the 1890s, poets were forced to acknowledge the obsolescence of existing poetic forms and adopted conventions of popular culture. Although many expected poetry to disappear in the wake of mass-circulation magazines and genre fiction, it adapted successfully to the changing circumstances (Newcomb 2004: xxv, 57).

Artists, of course, feared the encroachment of the market and of politics on their studios, creating for them conditions of dependence. But they engaged both out of necessity, as Pierre Bourdieu shows in his investigation of French cultural life in the late nineteenth century. And they did so in order to preserve the autonomous sphere of art—that is the right to determine the rules of art's own legitimacy. The conflict between the autonomous province of art, on the one hand, and the imperium of power and emporium of money, on the other, had come to define the artists and the intellectual. Thus at the time that writers, like Flaubert and Gautier, were denouncing bourgeois art and protecting the exclusive right of artists to judge art, they were entering the political world. It is, of course, a paradox that at the end of the nineteenth century "when the literary field, the artistic field, and the scientific field arrive at autonomy, that the most autonomous agents of these autonomous fields intervene in the political field as intellectuals." That is, they penetrate the domain of politics not as writers transformed into politicians but as intellectuals, "with an authority founded on the autonomy of the field and all the values associated with it: ethical purity, specific expertise" (Bourdieu 1995: 342).[22] They took controversial political positions and fought for unpopular causes because, as specialists in the areas of culture, they could look critically at their society.

The defense of autonomy became heated at the end of the nineteenth and beginning of the twentieth centuries, that is, the period of modernism, due to the deepened interpenetration of the realm of art and learning with the realms of money and politics. This tendency has only intensified with the consolidation of the culture industry, creating serious problems of dependence for intellectuals and artists alike. The challenge today, Bourdieu affirms, is to continue the struggle for the preservation of autonomy. Artists and intellectuals must fight for the "separation from heteronomous producers" and guarantee "culture producers the economic and social conditions of autonomy in relations to all forms of power" while at the same time avoiding the temptation to remain in the ivory tower (1995: 347–48).

Only Autonomous Art Can be Political

Intellectuals and artists have been engaging in this battle for at least two hundred years, ever since the rise of art as a separate institution.[23] They have sought a sovereign space, albeit an imaginary one, from which to reflect on society. That this autonomy was symbolic does not mean it was inconsequential. The idea that the art world was free of social and state control opened up a conceptual forum in society from which artists and intellectuals were able to criticize a host of oppressive systems from absolutism to capitalism, from sexism to imperialism. The exercise of intellectual freedom was primarily an aesthetic enterprise, based on the call that art should be free, originally from the priest, the prince, and then from the entrepreneur, the police, and the bureaucrat. In other words, the capacity of intellectuals to evaluate reigning social, cultural, and political norms was ensured by the dominion originally declared for art.

These artists, poets, and theorists could condemn political absolutism or neoclassicism by resorting to arguments of autonomy, that is, by representing themselves as misfits or radicals, capable of overthrowing accepted norms.[24] They constituted the new sensuous and rebellious individual, eager to challenge the status quo (Gagnier 1994: 265). The synthesis that early German Romantics forged between art and politics was based on the hypothesis that only a new sensibility could make freedom a political reality (Blechman 1999: 23). But their belief in the uniqueness of the individual was not an exercise of narcissism for they wanted to fuse the self with the outside world, be this God, the state, the revolution, or nature. Primed on the Enlightenment and the French Revolution, they saw the emergence of a new person capable of enormous freedom. They extrapolated, Gerald N. Izenberg explains, the ideological foundation of revolutionary radicalism to novel claims about human autonomy, beyond anything available in political and social theory. These early romantics identified their own personal crises with the historical crisis of European history (1992: 50–51).

Today's attacks on aesthetic autonomy underestimate the historical value of this tradition. Taylor and Saarinen (1994), for instance, give this issue perfunctory treatment when they argue that the critical function of art does not presuppose an "Archimedean point" from which to observe and criticize society. Instead of offering an alternative to this "point," they simply state "it is necessary to develop strategies of criticism that develop available modes of production and reproduction" (Pedagogies 8). It is fair to ask how postmodernity conceives of social critique without some distance between the artist/intellectual and society, subject and object.

Romantic artists engaged in this critique from the perch of culture. But we cannot appreciate this if we continue to see aesthetic autonomy as a withdrawal from life.[25] Writers who focus on "inwardness" fail to grasp that the institutionalization of art was accompanied by politicization of the artist. Indeed, the growing independence of art was linked to the "bourgeois consciousness of freedom" and the struggle for political sovereignty (Adorno 1997: 225). Habermas has shown that the social category of the intellectual arose in the public sphere of the eighteenth century largely through discussions of literature and democracy. John McGowan rightly calls this new social class "democracy's children" because they were interested in questions of freedom, political rights, and governance (2002: xi).[26] Scrutinizing society from the vantage point of culture, they were in a sense entangled in and profited from this nexus of power and culture.

If we examine this connection between politics and aesthetics, we find that a new conceptual and institutional space opened up in the eighteenth century that challenged the old regime. The organs of this space—the periodical, newspaper, novel, journalist, critic, music concert, theater, and museum—were all cultural (Blanning 2002: 2). The emergence of these agents and structures, along with the appearance of the sense of public opinion, constituted a cultural revolution whose impact was felt in the realm of politics.

Of course, not every artist or intellectual was a revolutionary. Many, however, were inspired by the possibility of political and social transformation. This is particularly true of German intellectuals who have been historically maligned for their indifference to social struggles. But these intellectuals were more "political than those of any other European country" (Blanning 211). For early Romantics aesthetics and politics were inseparable (Beiser 1996: xii–xiii). They gave enthusiastic support to the French Revolution until the late 1790s, and the revolution dominated German philosophy during that decade. Many were active in local government, and a few, like Fichte and Hölderlin, were involved in seditious activities. Late Romantics, disillusioned by the violence of the French Revolution and with the possibility of emancipation, took a conservative turn. Rather than linking art to politics, they substituted art for politics, striving for an aesthetic rather than for a political revolution.[27] But their precursors were fervent believers in social change. Friedrich Hölderlin's passion for the Greek struggle against the Ottoman Empire bears this out. Even as he mourned the departure of ancient Hellas, he was an enthusiastic supporter of independence for modern Greece.[28]

The Greek war of independence, which received global attention, demonstrates intense artistic involvement in politics. Dionysios Solomos dramatized the Greek revolution in his lyrics; Lord Byron abandoned an aristocratic life in England to fight for the Greek cause and died in the battle of Missolongi; Eugene Delacroix completed a number of paintings on the Greek revolution to enlist sympathy for the rebellious Greeks.[29]

The Greek case has been repeated countless times in the history of art since then. In an exhaustive study of the relationship between social radicalism and the arts in Europe from the French Revolution to 1968, Donald Drew Egbert has charted a story of artists alienated first by absolute monarchies and then by capitalist bourgeoisie who sought to transform society (1970). The artist's activist role can also be seen in the postcolonial struggles. Artists have played a leading role in decolonization as attested by José Carlos Mariátequi, (1971), Ngugi Wa Thiong'o (1972, 1981), and Chinweizu and Madubuike (1983). They were engaged in the fashioning of a resistance literature, which emerged as part of the organized national liberation struggles (Harlow 1987: xvii).

None of this is new, of course. But an important lesson rises from these lists: *Only autonomous art can be oppositional.* A pile of bricks in the hardware store conducts no criticism because it fulfills its representational and utilitarian functions. A brick is a brick is a brick. But in the gallery the brick's utility is denied, relieved of normal usage. It turns into metaphor. A brick is not a brick is a texture is a color is a house is a memory is a smell of lentil soup.

Art is metamorphosis, the craft of making changes. It imagines the impossible and inconceivable because of its endlessly analogical potential. "In this metaphorical alchemy," Jay Parini writes, "changes occur and they seem true" (2008: 77). But what does this have to do with revolution? The answer is that art is political by simply being there. That is to say, art is political not only in terms of its contents—the representation of war or the positions taken by artists—but also in terms of its autonomous structure. It "criticizes society by merely existing," as Adorno knew (1997: 226). Art engages in politics by fencing off its lot as unreality or antireality, a place of illusions, lies, reflections, stray paths, and half-seen faces. It invites us to interact with our world by letting us step out of it, if only for an exhilarating second.

§4 Art as Parabasis

"A thing is incredible only after it is told—returned to the world it came out of."

—Eudora Welty, "No Place for You, My Love"

What image best illustrates literature's autonomy in the world? Often I imagine it as a fence, dividing a field from an invented one, being part of each, yet also standing on its own. The fence signifies both the separation and the conjuncture of one patch with the other. Now and then I regard it as an eaves trough, projecting beyond the wall of a house but affixed to it. Running around the perimeter of the roof, the gutter collects rainwater while enjoying 360-degree views. Functional, it also strikes passersby with its copper hues. Other times I think of a spider web, fashioned between branches of two trees. While connected to them, it keeps its own shape. The web has its own integrity but would collapse without the support of the limbs. In all three cases, autonomy signifies an entity's dependence on the environment rather than its isolation. The object interacts with its milieu, separate from the world while communicating with it, self-directed but relational.

A common element in my three images is the line. Indeed, to talk about the uniqueness of something is to invoke the idea of boundaries, the differentiation of one place from the other. As John Dewey's work on experience helps us understand, "The aesthetic emotion is something distinctive but not cut off by a chasm from other and natural emotional experiences" (1934: 78). For Dewey experience results from the interaction of organism and environment, which transforms that reciprocity into "participation and communication" (22). Experience occurs continuously because the process of communication between self and milieu is part of living (35).

The aesthetic domain continuously communicates with its surrounds, maintaining a homeostasis while commingling with its environment.

Indeed, this dialogic process enables internal integrity. The transition from inside to the outside is imperceptible because the barrier resembles a moveable row of stones rather than a cement wall. The difference between interior and exterior is signified by these stones rather than by some physical property of the inside. Autonomy implies social procedures by which an entity posits dissimilarities between itself and the outside.[1]

Literature as Difference Between Reality and Nonreality

Like all other social systems then, literature lights up the fence marking itself from others. But unlike practical disciplines, like medicine or religion, literature is more heavily invested in bringing attention to this fence. Its raison d'être, so to speak, is to underscore the difference between life and fiction, highlighting itself as a place of and for simulation.

Literature takes pains to remind us that it peddles artifice and we, as readers, enjoy both the illusion and our consciousness of that illusion. It presents itself as fantasy by distinguishing its products from the outer world. In other words, literature's existence is tied up more in illuminating its uniqueness, its difference from life, than performing a utilitarian service, like mending broken bones or saving souls. Its status is paradoxical, its function not being functional in the practical sense, its influence not unmediated.

Literature's contradictory character makes it so hard for us to pin it down. Derek Attridge hints at this when he says that literature "is something *more* than the category or entity it is claimed to be (writing that has a particular institutional function . . .) and is valuable for something *other* than the various personal or social benefits that are ascribed to it" (2004: 5). But literature is also a tautology: the only vocation it could possibly claim for itself is hawking inventions because the capacity to discriminate between its alternate universe of fantasy and actuality is its only vocation.

Its representations stand for the world without ever disappearing into it because literature marks the difference between representation and reality. This is part of its circular makeup. "As a medium with its own mode of being," Geoffrey Hartman explains, literature "maintains a distance between itself and that reality" (Hartman 2002: 227). This distance is a component of literature's independent status. Literature touts itself as both a sovereign institution in the public realm and a separate mode of understanding the world. This double character refers to its historical existence as social practice (in the library, university, school, publishing house, newspaper) and to its aptitude in separating simulacra from actuality.

When I refer to this process of making distinctions, I take the Russian Formalist notion of defamiliarization one step further. While the Formalists argued that literature offers an offbeat, unconventional apprehension of reality, I suggest that it dramatizes and reinforces the gap between artifice and reality. As Victor Shklovsky outlines in "Art as Technique" (1917), literature works on the human faculty of perception. It makes us fully conscious of the world around us by intensifying our awareness of things so that we could become more responsive to them. It defamiliarizes the stuff of life, making the trodden path seem unexplored, the cliché unorthodox, the platitude unanticipated. Because the Formalists believed that literature frees our thoughts from the cobwebs of daily routine, they could argue that it made us live more deeply.[2]

In Joyce's *Stephen Hero*, Stephen Daedalus describes this intensity as epiphany—a "sudden spiritual manifestation" which is the duty of a "man of letters" to record "with extreme care." Stephen believes that the "clock of the Ballast Office was capable of an epiphany." The moment "the spiritual eye" focuses on it, the clock is "epiphanized" (1977: 188–89). When Stephen says that this object acquires the "supreme quality of beauty," he means that art turns everyday things into scenes of wonderment.

The Formalists were hardly the first to focus on literature's capacity to refresh our quotidian experiences. Many decades even before them, Shelley wrote that "poetry lifts the veil from the hidden beauty of the world, and makes familiar objects be as if they were not familiar" (1890: 13). With this observation he reinforced the Romantic conception of the imagination as a synthesizing, creative force. The function of the "poetical faculty" was to fashion "new materials of knowledge, and power, and pleasure" (38).

But Shklovsky refined this feature, turning it into the machine of literature. Defamiliarization, he argued, is found wherever form is found ([1917] 1965: 18). It is fundamental to riddles, word play, tropes, in short, to any mode of communication that places emphasis on the means of communicating through self-conscious use of figuration. The Formalists made a significant contribution to our understanding of literary function by showing that literature is concerned with the representation of the world but also with the mode of representation, its ultimate aim being to enhance our sensitivity to our environment, to make us pay attention. But there is something missing in their exploration of aesthetic function—its place in the world. The Formalists explained how literature refreshed daily perceptions without also defining its social context.

It is possible, however, to yoke the two, defamiliarization and aesthetic autonomy, into art's double character. Literature's capacity to prolong perception also brings light unto its own sovereignty, allowing readers to perceive both the aesthetic process and the artificiality of the represented object. Becoming aware of this operation, readers suspend, however fleetingly, their habitual identification with the object, glimpsing it from a new perspective. But by disrupting their identification with the real, literature *also* facilitates a distance between them and the real. It frustrates the human desire for unmediated communication, for the effortless entry into the actual. More than any other social practice, literature is characterized by a built-in mechanism to accentuate the threshold between itself and other spaces.

The significance of literature, therefore, extends beyond its capacity to make the familiar look bizarre. Its very existence, as an otherworldly domain, relentlessly reminds us of the boundary we draw between what we experience and what we imagine. "A thing is incredible only after it is told—returned to the world it came out of" says the narrator of Eudora Welty's haunting story "No Place for You, My Love" (1980: 480) Welty turns an afternoon jaunt into a descent through the netherworld of sexuality. But she also achieves something more, as she states in the line above, abandoning readers on that edge between undergoing an outing in a car and telling/reading about it.

How does Welty achieve this distancing effect? First she has two northerners, a (married) man and a (single) woman, who meet at a luncheon in New Orleans, drive off together through the sweaty, mosquito-buzzing landscape of the bayou to a vague destination. Powered by their own desire, they never exchange their names (1980: 480). "They were strangers to each other, both fairly well strangers to the place" (465). But it is also Welty's language—fluid, clammy, and sweltering—that takes the reader through this moist terrain. And then there is the tension between erotic and the internal logic of narration. The story's motion is propelled less by a stated goal—we don't know where they are going—than by sexual potential that is stronger than the landmarks of place.

Poised between self-possession and self-abandonment, the two characters speed forward, deeper and deeper into mystery that Sunday afternoon. They drive out into the "amphibious" land that appears red with flames. Sights of fishermen, girls with jet-black hair, "negroes" lounging on porches, wafting palmettos, trucks loaded with shrimp, and the levee flash by. The bugs leave the strongest impression, congealed as a thick mess on the windshield.

A tension binds the story, tying the predictable dialogue with unpredictable motion. Are they lost, we wonder? Why don't they talk about their lives or exchange telephone numbers? Are they going to meet again? What did they achieve with this flight? Does the ambiguous title, with its promise of intimacy, address them? Without knowing it, as the man and woman zoom through this land that is "south of South, below it," they slip into the underworld of their recognizable habitat. Like modern-day Euridice and Orpheus, they conduct their own *nekyia*, the mythological descent into Hades, the ancient journey of knowledge.

What they learn from this descent is unclear. When they return to the "deliberate imperviousness" of the hotel and their lives in Ohio and New York, they feel affected by something, having become more vulnerable perhaps. But this vulnerability has been brought about less by the drive itself than by the transformation of this outing into narrative. Their excursion becomes "incredible," to cite Welty again, only after it is told, in this case as fiction. Charles Baxter, writing about this distancing affect states that in fiction truth can be dramatic if its occurrence in real life is forgotten. Then the story can pull "something contradictory . . . out of its hiding place" (1997: 38). What is an issue here then is not the *nekyia* itself but the boldness it acquires later after it has been narrated. The tropes of fiction in this case, exaggeratedly sensual language, overloaded metaphorical descriptions of landscape—convert an afternoon drive into a journey along the frontiers of experience and narration. Welty uses the idea of sexual strain and enigma to convey the line between living and telling.

Of course, the story reworks the traditional boy-girl outing, as it also refreshes our views of the southern landscape. Beyond defamiliarizing our sense of an erotic encounter, however, Welty's text tests the link between the actual and imagined. For an experience to make sense, Welty's narrator writes, it has to be reconnected to the real by being retold, converted into fiction. It can be considered "incredible" if it is related to someone on the other side, returned back to where the teller originated.

The couple in her narrative will recount their odyssey, "that strangers, they had ridden down into an extraordinary land together and were getting safely back—by a slight margin, perhaps, but margin enough" (1980: 480). Welty's story brings attention to the *margin* between strangeness and nonstrangeness, the rim between an experience and a fable, the edge separating the drive into the bayou from its subsequent fictionalization.[3]

Literature as Boundary

This margin between the real and invented is always arbitrary and blurry. But Welty suggests that it will always be here and that the task of literature is to remind us of it. We need the incredible just as we need the opportunities to differentiate between a story and an unstory. There is a tautology here, as I noted earlier. Literature ensures that this border marking will be maintained as a social good. But in order for literature to watch over this boundary, it must retain its own distance from reality. It brings light to the gap between fiction and reality because it also needs this gap to live.

Consider the protagonist Neddy Merrill in John Cheever's story, "The Swimmer." He comes to think about the distinction between truth and illusion when he decides to return home from a friend's house by swimming through all the pools along the eight-mile route. "Making his way home by an uncommon route gave him the feeling that he was a pilgrim, an explorer, a man with a destiny" (1978: 715).

Cheever's text exploits two key conventions of the short story: focus on one act and one character so as to gain access into that man's mind. In one respect it seems improbable that a person could blithely dip into every pool over a course of many miles until he reaches his own. What makes the story work as fiction, however, is the integrity it fosters between this watery journey and the self-examination Teddy undergoes, a process told in a language deceptively diaphanous. Yet, the clarity of the prose obscures a raw truth. For as Teddy approaches his destination, he comes to realize what he has so far succeeded in denying, namely that he has lost his fortune and has had to sell his house. So when, as a suburban Odysseus, he arrives at Ithaca, he finds his home locked up and empty. But this self-discovery becomes possible once he lunges into the unsettling river of pools, a world that is an aesthetic fantasy. Only by fictionalizing his odyssey can he discover his real life as illusion.

By bordering itself off as a place of semblance, the short story presents its narrative as separate from the world. But in claiming truth-value for its representations, it draws a link between itself and that world. We have the simultaneous embrace of autonomy and rootedness, that Gemini quality I have been describing. But what happens in the process is an interaction between semblance and actuality, art and not-art rather than the folding of one into another. Such a collapse would lead to what Robert Kaufmann refers to as "aestheticist delusion," the inability to differentiate between identities and between "art work and world" (2008: 210). It is literature (and art in general) that both sustains the boundary between fact and fiction and accentuates the indispensability of this boundary.

Readers of a newspaper, for instance, would grow impatient with an article written in the intense figuration of lyric, sacrificing content to achieve literary effect. They would not appreciate a computer manual published as a short story. Nor would they take kindly to a letter from a friend parading as fiction. We need this correspondence to be authentic since our relationship with our friend depends on truthful revelation. A short story, on the other hand, could easily take the form of an epistle, as does John Updike's epistolary "Dear Alexandros" (1973).

In the first letter, Alexandros, a Greek orphan, writes to a Mr. and Mrs. Brentley in Greenwich, New York, thanking them for adopting him as a foster son through the charity, Hope International. The English of the text conveys a child's tone and the broken idiom of translation. The reply by Kenneth Brently is self-assured and fluent, revealing an educated man of means. But the relationship between the two is transformed by the revelation that Mr. Bentley is forced to make to guileless Alexandros, namely that he has separated from his wife and has been living with another woman since his last note. In trying to explain to his young correspondent the state of his marriage, he imagines Alexandros wondering if the Brentleys have been telling him lies or perhaps lying to each other. As crucial as this question is for understanding Mr. Bentley's character, however, the more important one is the question the story asks about fiction. Are the lies of the letter the same as the lies of the story? What is the difference between personal correspondence and a work of fiction? Or, as Updike asks again in "Packed Dirt, Churchgoing, a Dying Cat, a Traded Car," how can you tell whether the text in your hand is a short story or an essay?

The protagonist of that story, David Kern, is a writer who picks up a hitchhiker on his way to his sick father in Philadelphia. When asked by the young sailor why he writes, the narrator answers inconclusively. Only after he visits his dying father does he come to an understanding about his craft: Writing is a social activity, a communal effort in finding aesthetic meaning within everyday acts. Or rather, it is a process of discrimination, a way of differentiating the special from the ordinary. In a society devoid of rituals, art brushes up certain events, people, and things, setting them slightly apart. In his mind later, he answers the hitchhiker: "We in America need ceremonies, is I suppose, sailor, the point of what I have written" (1973: 279).

What David would have said to the sailor had they returned together is that literature defamiliarizes life. Through its special tropes it brings light to the forgotten or little-noticed occurrences, things, and people. He comes to this realization by recollecting a series of events that he previously had dismissed in the randomness and routine of life—a cat in Oxford, his first car, and the father's long illness. Everything in his life dissolved back "into the mineral world," like the dead animal. The elements in the story's title—packed dirt, churchgoing, a dying cat, and a traded car had receded into near oblivion. David had simply passed by them without fanfare. It is art that pays respect to the "sight of bare earth that has been smoothed and packed firm by the passage of human feet" (246).

While the story celebrates the power of art to enhance our perception of events and people, it also does something that ironically escapes David's notice—it refracts these experiences. It challenges us, in other words, to think about the transition from semblance to truth and back again. Updike's story achieves this in form and content. As a work of fiction, Updike's text tries to pass itself as both a memoir where the author reflects on significant events in his life and an analytical essay where the author tries to figure out the place of art in life. This masquerade, however, can only take place if we accept it first and foremost as a short story exploiting both the conventions specific to this genre and the wider convention of art as peddler of illusions.

The Literary Difference

This is the social benefit of literature: its mere existence. By preserving the border between an aesthetic and an empirical order, it enables us to take a distance from this reality, criticize it, and ultimately change it. It is fair to ask, then, how literature achieves this. This question, going to the core of art's function, cannot be answered generally, of course, because every art operates according to its own logic. Even within literature each genre has formal properties that distinguish it from the other modes of writing.[4]

We have come to understand that, by exploiting figuration, literature accentuates for readers its distance from reality. Traditionally critics have thought of this as literature's formalism. Structuralism referred to it as literariness whereas deconstruction characterized it as metaphoricity. More recently, critics have spoken about the performative quality of literature (Hillis Miller 2002: 37; Gourgouris 2003: 10).

What critics have meant by these varying concepts is that literature heats up the denotative nature of language to make the sign signify something else, to delay meaning. While in ordinary language the signifier signals its difference from the signified, in literature, it endures further differentiation. This is why readers of literature end up feeling that something has escaped them or that the words blink in many directions at the same time. The signifier, Wolfgang Iser notes, is fictionalized, because what is said is not meant. This permits the signifier to be used in different ways. "If it no longer means what it denotes, then no longer meaning what it denotes becomes itself a denotation, bringing into existence something that does not yet exist" (1993: 248).

Literature, of course, is not unique in this. Advertising and rhetoric are performative in their own ways as they also bring attention to the medium of communication. So does the pastime of play. Observing two monkeys play-fight in the San Francisco zoo, Gregory Bateson concluded that these animals were capable of metacommunication to a certain extent, aware that the nip was not really a bite but something else, a form of play. "These actions in which we now engage [combat] do not denote what those actions for *which they stand* would denote" (1972: 180). In other words, the fight is not real but a sign for something else. The play ends in a fight when one participant crosses this line or when the other misunderstands a particular action. Then the nip is indeed a bite that draws blood. In this case, the action has an impact on the empirical world that literature rarely achieves.[5]

The uniqueness of literature then lies less in its self-conscious deployment of figuration, however important this quality, than in the way it exploits this deployment to make the audience aware of the distinction between a combat and its representation, a monopoly game and the *real* estate market. The ultimate distinctiveness of literature exists in the type of performance it carries out—maintaining the boundaries between semblance and actuality. Denis Donoghue expresses this succinctly when he argues that literature makes counterstatements to society "not discursively but formally: as particular forms to be apprehended, achievements of invention and style, the right words in the right order, proprieties of cadence and invention" (2003: 114). Literature sets itself opposite of society, not necessarily against it, in order to provide alternate versions of society.

This "counter-factual" quality endows literature's statements with artfulness, which, in turn, enhances their otherworldliness. I believe this is what Herman Melville means when he reflects on the place of fact-based writing in fiction. "The symmetry of form attainable in pure fiction cannot so readily be achieved in a narration essentially having less to do with fable than with fact," he says in *Billy Budd, Sailor*. "Truth uncompromisingly told will always have its ragged edges; hence the conclusion of such a narration is apt to be less finished than an architectural finial" (1962: 128). Self-conscious artistry, he suggests, turns a narration into something fabulous and manufactured. This artfulness (Donoghue's "properties" of invention) brings to the fore the experience of fabrication while highlighting the gap between truth and fable.

What is at issue here is less this distance between fact and fiction than literature's view of itself as a manufacturing process. It marks itself off primarily as an artifice-promoting space that cannot disappear into the natural world. "In contrast to all other modes of production," Heidegger argued, "the work [of art] is distinguished by being created so that its createdness is part of the created work" (1971: 62). Its artificiality, in other words, constitutes its very identity, even—to use an example from modern visual arts—when it comes already formed, like a pile of bricks. Art assumes this aura of a constructed product in the art gallery. "The work of art is an artificial object," commented Le Corbusier (Charles-Édouard Jeanneret) and Amédée Ozenfant, ([1929] 1964: 58). Its fake nature, which Schiller characterized as its sentimentality, presupposes and promotes a gap from the empirical world. Schiller saw this as the feature of functionally differentiated art but perhaps all art is sentimental. That is to say, all art is conscious of itself as cut off from the object it seeks to represent. The trick behind Zeuxis's painting of grapes only works when compared with the real grapes the birds longed to eat.[6] People take delight in self-conscious semblance. A trompe l'oeil, then, charms viewers when its illusions become apparent, when they realize the disparity between the actual object and its reproductions.

My argument here does not rehash the traditional opposition between fiction and reality, which sees fiction as the opposite of reality. I do not pose reality as a given empirical order we simply perceive and discover, even in the cognitive misalignment the Formalists spoke of. Rather, I maintain that, *historically* in conditions of autonomy, literature has turned the relationship between actual world and invention into a main preoccupation. In so doing, it transforms this relationship into an epistemological and aesthetic dynamic.

Hardly a trivial exercise, literature's capacity to make us engage with the dialectic between the empirical and the real is an essential good in society. By remaining vigilant at the border of fact and fable, literature holds off the pressure to fold one into the other. Thus, even if literature may not be able to affect the empirical universe, it provides a vital "service," which is not a service in the regular sense because it points to and guards a border, a difference. And this function rises from the boundary literature drew historically around its own space. Its capacity to misalign experience is directly related to its structural sovereignty, that is, to the gap it presupposes between itself and nature. This is what I have been calling the art's twin character, that it is both autonomous structure and, what Adorno referred to as a "fait social" (social fact) (1997: 252).

This distancing enables readers to maintain some clearance from reality, reflect on that reality, and then change it. Although literature itself does not transform the world, it fosters a cognitive perspective that enables both critique and real-life impact. "The imaginary world of art," Luhmann notes, "offers a position from which *something else* can be determined *as reality*. . . . Without such markings of difference, the world would simply be the way it is. Only when a reality 'out there' is distinguished from fictional reality can one observe one side from the perspective of the other" (2000: 142). In other words, the cosmos fashioned by art offers us a standing point from which both to observe our own social cosmos and transform it. By encouraging the maximum use of fabrication while defending its space as an abode for fabrication, literature creates an alternate universe that makes sense only as a juxtaposition to the real one. Traditionally this capacity has been called creativity, the freedom we experience in art, when we find ourselves no longer bound by the rules of signification, gravity, law, or religion. This latitude encourages us to take a flight of fancy while being conscious of the here and now.[7]

The Leeway of Literature

The simultaneous push and pull of fantasy and participation comes out in Raymond Carver's story, "Cathedral" (1983). Carver shows that art not only puts the quotidian in a different light—pulling down the ivy from ancient stone but also creates for us the possibility of grasping something we had not pictured before—a cathedral. Carver achieves this both through the narrated story but also through the mode of narration. Composed in his minimalist style, the writing seems Cavafian in its bareness, so devoid of metaphors, even ordinary adjectives. The story is told in a distancing, chilly, matter-of-fact voice. "The blind man, an old friend of my wife's, he was on his way to spend the night. His wife had died" (209). It is almost deliberately "artless," defying anyone to take it as literature. There is a sense that this story is "uncompromisingly told," to cite Melville again, that we are dealing with something still waiting to be fashioned. But then it lassoes the reader, both with the deceptive simplicity of its style and the revelation of character.

The story begins when the unnamed narrator explains that Robert, a blind friend of his wife, would spend the night with them. As we learn of his reactions to this visit, starting with the declarative "A blind man in my house was not something I looked forward to" (1983: 209), we come to know him as an unimaginative, unfeeling person, fearing contact with people. Our view is confirmed when, whether through thoughtlessness or sardonic humor, he asks his guest on which side of the train he sat. The narrator tries to resist Robert's entry into his life just as we guard against his cold solitude. Only gradually do we warm to him.

The turning point occurs when the narrator, again either out of insensitivity or gracelessness, turns on the television to a documentary on cathedrals. Without the mediation of his wife who has gone to bed, the narrator has to confront Robert's blindness and, of course, his own blinkered state. In a sense, he is Oedipus who sees but does not know the truth, talking to the blind Teiresias, who can't see but knows. Little by little, he opens up to Robert, accepts his guest and sympathizes with him. At one point, he asks Robert: "Do you have any idea what a cathedral is? What it looks like, that is? . . . If someone says cathedral to you, do you have any notion what they're talking about?" (224). But Robert can't associate any images with the word other than the number of years it took to build them. He asks his host to describe one to him. Trying hard to do this, "as if my life depended on it" (225), the narrator has to resort to visual description. But at the end, he gives up.

Feeling his host's frustration, Robert suggests that they draw one together. He sends him for pens and heavy paper. The narrator returns with an old shopping bag, shakes the dried onionskins out and flattens it out on the floor. With both of them on the carpet, he takes Robert by the hand and presses the pen down hard on the paper to create the profile of a cathedral. After awhile Robert takes the lead, asking the narrator to close his eyes. "His fingers rode my fingers as my hand went over the paper. It was like nothing else in my life up to now." Working together, they form a cathedral that probably does not correspond to anything in real life. But they both know it's a cathedral because they can see/feel it, a figure pressed upon a used bag.

The story dramatizes what I referred to earlier as the denotative property of literature. Here quite literally the word *cathedral* does not connote a fixed mental image. Rather it is made to stand for something else, an impression on a paper bag. In trying to figure this out, in drawing together this picture of the word, the two men emphasize the communal process of creation.[8] Carver's text enacts not so much the scene of writing, as deconstruction would put it, as the drama of aesthetic construction. In so far as the narrator and Robert conceive of what a cathedral might look like, they put into practice the Aristotelian definition of poetic composition. The function of poetry, Aristotle explains in the *Poetics*, is to describe, "not the thing that has happened, but a kind of thing that might happen." Poetry is superior to other modes of writing in that "its statements are of the nature rather of universals, whereas those of history are singular" (1984: 2323 [1451b1]).[9] The communication finally achieved by both characters is essentially aesthetic in nature. They come to know each other by drawing a church. If literature offers a way of knowing the world, it attains this by analogy rather than by mimesis by making something stand for something else and getting someone to stand in someone else's shoes, as Kant understood.[10]

Carver's narrator touches someone for the first time. Just as important, he learns the importance of make-believe, of imagining novel possibilities. Together he and Robert conceive of something that is fanciful and actual. The outline of this edifice is really only a matter of pressure, the difference between a fissure scraped on the paper and the surface of that paper. But this border between substance and emptiness, depth and flatness, is only a division between a cathedral and a noncathedral.

In arriving at this understanding the narrator discovers another form of literary truth, what I would call aesthetic empathy. He has come to see the world through someone else's eyes, by undergoing provisional blindness. To the extent that literary writing energizes the denotative tendency of language, it encourages this capacity in people to identify with others. In narrative, Mark Turner explains, we are able to project one story upon another and change our point of view, ultimately creating spaces for someone else's position (1996: 118).

Carver's story suggests that the ability to substitute one's self with the other is fundamentally an aesthetic experience. Literary works "typically invite readers to put themselves in the place of people of many different kinds and to take on their experiences" (Nussbaum 1995: 5). They give them access into someone else's thinking. We read novels, David Lodge points out, because they provide us with a convincing sense of what the consciousness of people other than ourselves is like (2002: 30).[11] Yet, our identification with the other does not in itself lead to a seamless union because the embrace is never complete, because of literature's capacity to distance us from the world.

Literature, as I have argued in the previous chapter, is political not just by representing injustice (thematics) but also by fostering a detachment from this injustice (structure). We empathize with the young narrator in Richard Wright's 1937 autobiography, *Black Boy*, but the mimetic quality of the prose compels us to step back in horror from the Jim Crow South it describes. The brilliance of the work, which has the narrative sweep of a novel, is to show in minute detail how violence and racism forced African Americans to dissimulate in order to survive.[12] Richard Wright constantly has to maneuver between his own feelings and thoughts and the external white world. Every time he meets a white man in Jackson, Mississippi, and later in Memphis, Tennessee, he wonders how best to react. Should he keep his head down? Should he smile? If asked a question, should he speak? What are the man's intentions? Is he trying to trap him? Growing up he learns never to reveal his true self to whites. He manages this inside/outside dichotomy of the self through strategies of deception and concealment.

But these strategies of the person are paralleled in the dissimulation of literary writing. As young Richard comes to learn that staying alive depends on knowing the difference between reality and fiction, he discovers how literary fiction works. Literature offered him the purchase to jump out of his horror. Having deceived the librarian in Memphis to allow him library privileges, he begins to read what had been forbidden. "It had been my accidental reading of fiction and literary criticism that had evoked in me vague glimpses of life's possibilities," works that were "critical of the straitened American environment." The "imaginative constructions" in the novels and stories give him the discourse and the tools to take "action" (1937: 227).

Wright is referring here not to the traditional sense of enlightenment, namely, that books opened his eyes to the world. Twain, Zola, Gogol, and Gide did not have to teach him about oppression. Rather, it was literature's double character, its capacity to be in the world while also hovering outside it, that enabled him to comprehend his own double consciousness as an African American in the South. The tensions literature incorporates between reality and its reconstruction allowed Wright, a "black boy" and "nigger," to find glimpses of "faint promise." The disjuncture of literature coincided with the disjuncture of his life, and this lack of fit became for him the basis for action.

Of course, not all art is revolutionary or subversive. That would be a predictable and easy argument but an inaccurate one. A particular aesthetic tradition can become itself sclerotic, as it can also be used by political regimes for repressive purposes. In short, I don't articulate a crude one-to-one correspondence between the word and the act. Rather I claim that literature preserves its own dominion, as it also fosters a degree of aloofness among readers. Herein lies its political potential: the capacity it instills in its audience to create counterstatements is dependent on its own social autonomy. Art's political impulse, Herbert Marcuse argued, lies in its aesthetic dimension, in the sovereign space where experience is refracted and subverted. When art abandons this autonomy, it succumbs to the reality it seeks to address (1978: 6, 49). What this would result in is a mimetic delusion I spoke of earlier, the collapse of identities into one another.

The modern artist who most internalized this self-conscious distancing is, of course, Bertolt Brecht. As Adorno noted, Brecht "found that to give his political position artistic expression it was necessary to distance himself from that social reality at which his works took aim" (Adorno 1997: 226). Brecht's ultimate purpose was to create a political theater that would contribute to social change. Epic theater, he insisted, shows "man himself as dependent on certain political and economic factors and at the same time as capable of altering them" (1957: 86). For such a stage to achieve this social transformation it had to defamiliarize the theatrical experience, to undermine the expectations of the audience.

The point of this alienation effect or *Entfremdung*, which he defined as "turning the object of which one is to be made aware . . . from something ordinary, familiar, immediately accessible, into something peculiar, striking, and unexpected" (143), was to prevent the audience from taking the play for granted, from assuming it to be natural. Specifically, this meant actors had to frustrate the audience's wish to identify with the characters on stage (193). In epic theater there must be "no illusion that the player is identical with the character and the performance with the play" (195).

Brecht's theory and theater perform art's dual referentiality. Art claims authenticity by aggravating the audience's desire for mimesis and by emphasizing the staged nature of its authenticity. As such, art for Brecht is both entertainment and action/pedagogy, aiming at aesthetic pleasure as well as real-life impact (135, 180).

Parabasis

This crucial link between politics and art, the real and nonreal, is dramatized with fury in Athenian Old Comedy, specifically in the section known as the parabasis.[13] In this segment of the play—usually made up of seven parts, each following prescribed rules of Greek meter—members of the chorus step off the stage, remove their masks and costumes, to address the audience on matters of social, cultural, and political import. Historically they often pointed directly to Athenian politicians and personalities sitting in front, mocking them while chastising the audience for having elected such idiots. These episodes often constituted unbridled ad hominem attacks on contemporaneous personalities. At times the chorus assaulted the audience's aesthetic tastes, as in Aristophanes' "Wasps," where the chorus complained that his "Clouds" had not been given first prize in the previous competition.[14]

Now once again, spectators, if you love
To hear plain speaking, pay attention, please!
The author has a bone to pick with you
For treating him unfairly. (1964: 75)

What takes place in the parabasis is not satire but unrestrained political criticism conducted in the context of art, "licensed ridicule and abuse of individuals" (Dover 1993: 247). The parabasis accomplishes its critique by violating the boundary between stage and viewer, thereby affirming to the spectators that the work before them is both illusion and real. Perhaps more than any other feature of art, the parabasis asserts the idea that artificiality is part of art's self-presentation. It certainly goes beyond Brecht's notion of alienation in refusing to allow members of the audience to identify with the illusion.

Stemming from the verb *parabaino* (to overstep or pass over), the parabasis is literally a transgression or digression that interrupts the dramatic action, abandoning the make-believe of theater. Even though the plays of Aristophanes have predominantly contemporaneous and socially relevant topics such as peace and war in the "Acharnians," peace and women in "Lysistrata," and education in the "Clouds," the parabasis punctures the curtain of fantasy by speaking about the here and now. What is distinctive of the parabasis, according to Thomas K. Hubbard, is its "simultaneous digressiveness and integration with the dramatic events" (1991: 2). As such, it is central to the drama's "cognitive self-realization as both a literary and social event" (17). By breaking down the fantasy of art, it makes the spectators part of the spectacle.

Addressing the audience openly, the parabasis insinuates itself into the community, presenting itself as both aesthetic effect and political intervention. By crossing a line on the stage without stepping off it, the parabasis highlights the connection between representation and social action, dramatizing in this way the relationship between aesthetic form and civic life. It affirms art as a social phenomenon, neither entirely separate from, nor an uninterrupted continuation of life. But the parabasis is only semi-autonomous, as it depends on the play for its effect. Without the drama, it would appear as a political tract, however well crafted, delivered in the Assembly. Yet, free of references to contemporaneous events, indictments of state figures, and roasting of the spectators, it would be an ordinary comedy, albeit one preoccupied with political events.

By taking place within the confines of art, using the language and meter of poetry, it delivers a harsh critique. This appraisal is politically palatable because it is declaimed in poetic discourse, which, as art, can disclaim real-life impact. But its effect is made possible by the conventions of drama and by the social reality around the theater of Dionysus, that is, war, incompetent leaders, lazy bureaucrats, self-aggrandizing orators, and gullible spectators. The parabasis is part art, part politics at the same time, participating in the political debate as a work of art. No one could mistake the one for the other, falling in this way into mimetic delusion.

Aristophanes' "Acharnians," his oldest extant play, which won first prize in 425 BCE, shows how the parabasis functions. The chief protagonist, Dicaiopolis, his name meaning just city, is a farmer tired of the war, who decides to conclude his own private treaty with Sparta. Confronted by an angry mob of charcoal burners, the Acharnians, who represent the war party and play the part of the chorus, Dicaiopolis addresses them outside the Pnyx, the Athenian Assembly, as he waits impatiently for the politicians chattering in the Agora. But rather than delivering a political speech, he assumes the role of Telephus from Euripides' eponymous play. He underscores, in this way, the dual meaning of spectatorship inherent in the play, the political and theatrical (Dobrov 2001: 45). Running into Euripides, he asks the tragedian to lend him Telephus's rags. "The audience has got to know who I am, but the Chorus has got to be fooled, at least until my telling Telephean phrases have knocked them into the middle of next week" (Aristophanes 1973: 69).

The citizen, who wanted to hear the rhetoric in the Pnyx, now becomes an actor himself, delivering a speech within a play. The passive spectator of both politics and the stage turns active citizen:

Don't hold it against me, gentlemen, if, though a beggar—and a comic poet at that—I make bold to speak to the great Athenian people about matters of state. Not even a comedian can be completely unconcerned with truth and justice; and what I am going to say may be unpalatable, but it's the truth. At least this time I can speak freely, with no risk of being charged by Cleon with slandering the City in the presence of foreigners. (71)

Dicaiopolis proclaims the ability of comedy to deliver the unvarnished truth about the war between Athens and Sparta that erupted in 431 BCE and did not end until 404 with some intervals of peace in between. Here he refers openly to Cleon, the politician who most favored the continued conflict with Sparta and scuttled an opportunity in 425 for an honorable peace. He had also prosecuted Aristophanes a year earlier on the grounds of slandering the state with his production of "The Babylonians." Dicaiopolis, speaking as Aristophanes himself, affirms the capacity of art to undertake political criticism because it is art, that is, not political discourse.

To be sure, he feels safe to conduct his diatribe against the city's leaders only in the guise of a theatrical character—art's secret weapon to avoid censorship through the ages. In so doing, he brings attention to the overlap between aesthetic form and civic life.

Then it is the Acharnians' turn to speak. They remove their masks and, now no longer spectators to Dicaiopolis's performance, address the Athenian public in the Theater of Dionysus, which was not far from the Pnyx itself. They begin their parabasis by referring to the link between literature and politics:

> He has won the debate and converted the State
> (At least, so we hope) to his view.
> Now let's strip for the dance and make use of our chance
> To convey our opinions to you. (77)

They remind the audience that since Aristophanes had started writing comedies, he has never used his parabasis to say that he is "clever." But now that he has been charged with slandering the state, "he wants to find / If, true to your tradition, you since then have changed your mind" (77). But all he did was tell the Athenians the truth (78). The chorus leader lashes out at Creon:

> So, though Cleon may itch
> For another big fight,
> He will never prevail,
> For justice and right
> Are my allies. (79)

It is impossible to disentangle art from society, theater from politics. The parabasis here functions as a metaphor, suggesting that art dramatizes the tension between illusion and the empirical world without at all separating one from another.

This is hysterically demonstrated in "The Frogs," first staged in 405 BCE and Aristophanes' last surviving work. As a whole, the play concerns the waning of Athenian drama and the weakening of the Athenian city-state. While the parabasis enacts the political function of poetry, the play explores the place of poetry in society. The play begins with Dionysus, the god in whose honor the dramatic festivals were held, announcing that he is searching for a good poet to help the city in its political crisis (Aristophanes 1962: 486). He finally decides to descend to Hades, along with his slave, Xanthias, to bring back the recently deceased Euripides as the city's savior, reenacting here in comic form the mythological *nekyia* that I spoke of earlier. At the end, he returns with Aeschylus after witnessing a dramatic agon between the two tragedians over who was the most accomplished artist.

Although the goal of the contest is to determine the best poet, the ultimate aim is political, to rescue the city. The artistic and political dimensions are mutually supportive of each other. As Dionysus says to the two poets, he came to the underworld to "help our city survive" so that it can continue to stage plays. "The one of you who has the best advice to give / for saving the city is the one that I'll take back" (577). By the time of the play's production, Athens had been involved in the conflict for about twenty-five years and suffered greatly as a result. A year later, the city was defeated, having lost its empire and its democratic institutions.

The chorus refers in the parabasis to these events, attacking politicians like Kleophon who supported the war: "Muse of the holy choruses . . . cast your eyes on this multitude of wits here seated / sharper than Kleophon, that sharper, on whose no-spik-Athenian beak / mutters bad pidgin-Attic" (531).[15] A few lines later it offers political advice, demanding amnesty for citizens and restoration of rights to those who lost them for political reasons: "It's the right and duty of our sacred chorus to determine / Better courses for our city." The chorus then turns to Kleigenes, "our current baboon" who "won't be around very long, and he knows it" (532). It ends the parabasis by exhorting the spectators to reject the current leadership and return to men of distinguished ancestry and proven worth (533). Having pressed the "foolish majority" to throw out the current leadership, the actors put on their masks and step back into the play.

In the meantime Dionysus decides to stage an agon, a rhetorical contest heard daily in the law courts and the assembly, between the patrician Aeschylus and the demotic Euripides. He proclaims an "agon sophias" ([a contest of wisdom] line 882) to decide "ten technen sophoteros" ([the wiser one in art] 780). Yet what takes place in this no-holds-barred duel is an examination of tragedy. It is interesting that tragedy is analyzed in the context of comedy, which turns out, here at least, to be the more metapoetic mode. Of the two, comedy has the greater leeway to exploit art's parabatic potential.[16]

Each poet irreverently attacks the other's work. Euripides accuses his rival of creating stodgy, unlifelike characters, bombastic style, and obscure prologues. "The chorus then would utter / four huge concatenations of verse. The characters just sat there mum" (544). He, on the other hand, made drama "democratic" by making dialogue "natural and conversational" (548). In contrast to Aeschylus's "massive constructions, huge words, and mountainous phrases" his characters talk like people (555). His plays are sleek, modern, and colloquial, relevant to contemporary life: "I turn everything inside out / looking for new solutions / to the problems of today," so that spectators questioned their lives and society as they left the theater (549).

Aeschylus, in his turn, blames Euripides for debasing tragedy with his "folksy style" (555). In Aeschylus's mind a poet is a teacher and preacher, exhorting his viewers to higher ground. Any man watching his "Seven Against Thebes" would "aspire to heroic endeavor" (552). Poets should rouse people to virtue, rather than corrupting them and filling them with lust (551). Euripides, on the other hand, has contributed to the softening of Athenian society. "You've emptied the wrestling yards of wrestlers. They all sit around on their fannies and listen to adolescent debates" (556).

Both poets continue picking out inconsistencies in each other's work and cases of flawed lyricism until Dionysus asks that scales be brought in to measure each poet's worth. This is perhaps the most preposterous moment of the play. The chorus itself is dismayed at this mercantile way of determining aesthetic value: "Had anyone else proceeded / to such invention / I would have said he needed / medical attention" (573). Even Dionysus recognizes the bathos of the act. "Bring out the scales then, if my duty is to judge / two master poets like a grocer selling cheese" (573). His slave, Xanthias and Hades's janitor, Aiakos, express misgivings as well, fearing this travesty shortchanges tragedy. Then Aiakos finally says "And they'll bring out their rulers and their angled rods, / and T-squares, the kind you fold" (538).[17]

Ultimately, it is not this farce that helps Dionysus determine the best poet but two political questions that he poses to each tragedian: (a) what to do about the brilliant statesman and general Alcibiades, now in self-imposed exile and (b) how to save Athens. The play ends there where it began, with the need to address the perilous situation of the polis. But it reflects on this condition through literature. The play concludes by returning to the start because it is entangled in a continuing rapport between art and life, poetry and politics.

Thematically, the play explores the significance of art to the polis by demonstrating that drama deals with issues of great import. Structurally, it accomplishes this by interrupting the dramatic action and forcing the spectators to turn around and laugh at their political leaders and themselves for electing them. While the characters *on the stage* may thrash out how poetry can come to the city's aid, the chorus *in the parabasis* steps out as a group of (not frogs, initiates, or inhabitants of Hades) citizens urging Athenians to action. At this moment, illusion stops and the play ceases being a play, however briefly. The bite, to return to my example of the mischievous monkeys, brings the play to a halt and becomes real. The actors cross the line to draw blood. Metacommunication is suspended and art seeks impact on the empirical world.

The parabasis shows how at certain historical junctures art may affect society, demonstrating what Jan Mukarovsky, said of the "aesthetic function": It is not a "mere, practically unimportant, epiphenomenon of other functions but is a co-determinant of human reaction to reality" ([1936] 1970: 95). Yet, the parabasis dramatizes something else that is unique to art, namely its capacity to highlight the curtain hanging between wispy fantasy of the stage and the rigid, marble seats of the audience, living and pretending, vision and refraction, what Pablo Neruda calls a crack "between shadow and space" (1970: 61).

§5 The Line Between Living and Pretending

"Nicht Trug! Die Bühne enthüllt uns das Geheimnis der Wirklichkeit."

—Richard Strauss, *Capriccio*[1]

Aristophanic comedy is a unique creation of an intensely politicized society that placed great value on the arts. The parabasis itself, bridging politics and art, stage and spectators, exemplifies this interaction between poetry and civic life. Aristophanes could, therefore, take for granted that his Athenian audience included officials, whom he lambasted. This situation of a compact city-state sponsoring a dramatic festival as a communal event of politicians, intellectuals, and commoners, cannot be easily reproduced elsewhere. It was, as Herder said of Athenian and Shakespearean tragedy, a product of its time. A contemporary playwright might introduce the parabatic into a work. But could she presume that the political elite, say of London or Toronto, would be in attendance?

Although the parabasis cannot be recreated exactly on stage, it has symbolic and explicatory potential for art. I believe that this formal feature of Athenian Old Comedy illustrates a property shared by literature in general—its capacity to highlight the tensions between autonomy and dependence. Moreover, it helps us demonstrate the social value of literature. Not just a trope, delighting in the potency of metaphor, the parabasis embodies the force of aesthetic function, a power that stems exactly from literature's limenal position between action and enactment.

Literature is about lines, says the native-Canadian writer Daniel David Moses. In a poem tellingly titled, "The Line," Moses plays with the idea of poetry as lines on paper and as a fishing line, drawing parallels between composing and angling. Is writing "this line I'm feeding you" nothing other than baiting readers? In the course of the text, Moses tries to define what poetry is by luring readers with an easy answer. But what we learn is: "the thought of what this line is / not is the weight that sinks it / in." Is it tropes, rhyme, rhythm, wit, words? But no line could be the poem. Moses makes the reading demanding by looping the sentences over to the next row of words, like the line in the water, causing a slight refraction in meaning. But readers can't really grab the hook. What they know with certainty is that poetry is a line itself between the reel and the real. How would you feel, the speaker asks, to discover that the poem might "lack the line to speak" (1900: np)?

So parabasis, as a historical phenomenon, exists only in fifth-century Athens. But the parabatic, the trait of literature drawing attention to the filament between fact and fancy, is everywhere, as Moses suggests. If that is the case, it is reasonable to ask, how the parabatic manifests itself outside of classical comedy.

All the Stage Is Parabasis

Perhaps the best place to start is the stage itself. Or is this too predictable? Theater stages so effortlessly the dynamic between the scene and those who see. But the exercise becomes more challenging if we begin with a tragedy by Aeschylus, who, according to Schiller, constitutes the last naïve poet. Generally associated with the birth of tragedy, Aeschylus would not normally be expected to display the "aesthetic" distance we see in Aristophanes, let alone the self-reflection of modern dramatists like Brecht and Peter Weiss. Yet, "The Persians," the earliest surviving Greek tragedy, incorporates the sense of art's constructedness discussed earlier. It presents itself as a work of literature, bringing together the "what has happened in the past" and the "what is happening now on the stage."

How does it achieve this dynamic without Aristophanic self-reflexivity? The simple answer is by being present. By dealing with contemporary events Aeschylus compelled viewers in 472 BCE to confront the simultaneous connect-disconnect between the representations of the Persians on stage and the impact the real Persians had on Athens eight years earlier.

The play was first performed eight years after the destruction of Athens by the Persians. As such, it is unique in Greek tragedy in treating contemporary events. Instead of dealing with mythological topics, Aeschylus focuses on the results of the Persian Wars (490, 480–479 BCE), when Athens emerged victorious in the battle of Salamis. Aeschylus, however, gives a twist to his representation. Rather than setting the play in his own native city to celebrate Athens' unexpected triumph, he chooses the Persian capital, Sousa, specifically, the court of Xerxes. Atossa, the mother of Xerxes and wife of the dead king, Darius, is in the palace anxiously waiting news about her son's expedition, who, angered by his father's defeat in the famous battle of Marathon in 490 BCE, had sought revenge for this national humiliation.

This decision to depict Persians on their own territory, rather than the gods or Homeric heroes, makes visible that edge between fact and fable. It forces the audience to confront both real and represented results of imperial aggression. But what the audience sees is not a simplistic portrayal of the Other as a one-dimensional enemy—the savage Indians in American westerns or the steely Germans in post-World War II movies. On the contrary, Aeschylus offers a relatively humane representation of the Persians. Although Aeschylus, who himself fought at the battles of Marathon and of Salamis, portrays the Greeks as militarily and culturally superior and ethnocentrically imposes upon the Persians an Athenian cultural and religious weltanschauung, he asks that his audience sympathize with the suffering of their enemies. The chorus of Persian elders sing of the misery visited upon the Persians: "Athens hateful to her foes. / Recall how many / Persians widowed vain, / And mothers losing sons" (Aeschylus 1956: 58). Later Aeschylus presents the scenes of lamentation of the Persians who have heard of the great loss at Salamis. The herald who delivers the tragic tidings to the Persian court describes the valor of the Persian warriors: "All the Persians, who were in nature's prime, / Excellent in soul, and nobly bred to grandeur, / Always first in trust, met their death / In infamy, dishonor, and in ugliness" (63). The chorus gives voice to the dignity and pathos of the Persian women, who sing their dirges, "rending their veils . . . / sharing their woe," softly weeping (66).

In so portraying the Persians as fellow human beings, Aeschylus highlights the capacity of literature to induce aesthetic sympathy in viewers. This is a remarkable challenge in itself considering that eight years earlier the Persians had ransacked and burned the city.[2] Seeking refuge on the island of Salamis across the bay, the Athenians could actually observe their city in flames.

Just as important, in attempting this reconciliation with Otherness, Aeschylus achieves a parabasis. Athenians watching his play in the theater of Dionysus could catch sight of the burned ruins on the Acropolis above them. As they listened to the dirges of the Persian women, they could turn their eyes slightly up to the left and behold the products of Persian violence. Athenians could not but ask whether there was a break between art and life. The play challenged them to rethink the line between the stage-set of Sousa in front of them and the wrecked buildings above them.

This parabasis is as historically determined as those by Aristophanes. In Aeschylus, however, although the illusion of the play is never interrupted directly, the immediate past and the present invade the play from the outside—in a reverse parabasis. It has to be assumed that the audience of the original production was made up of citizens who, like Aeschylus, had fought and/or had lost loved ones in the battles. The Athenian spectators were asked to traverse between a reality that was tragic and a tragedy that was real, between the anguish of the Persians and the suffering of the audience, enacted pain and the actual pathos. They could neither "surrender to reality" (in the words of the Swiss playwright Friedrich Dürrenmatt) and forget the agony and dignity of the foe nor capitulate to the stage and ignore the maimed citizens and charred ruins.

There is another parabatic moment, however, during which the play speaks to the audience directly about the dangers of power. As the ghost of Darius rises over the stage, it warns of the human capacity for hubris:

Remember Greece and Athens! Lest you disdain
Your present fortune, and lust after more,
Squandering great prosperity.
Zeus is the chastener of overboastful
Minds, a grievous corrector. (77).

Sixty years before Aristophanes' irreverent attack on (Athenian) imperial folly, Aeschylus delivers his own parabasis on the consequences of political domination. That Athenians had not paid attention to his warning, that they formed their own empire, which ultimately led to their own perdition, does not mitigate the force of the play to intercede in the civic life of the city. But this intervention is subtle and complex, involving literature's twin status as work of art and social occurrence. This double sidedness allows literature to perpetrate a real folly: it forces Athenian spectators to hear Persian lamentation and Persian warning about Athenian arrogance. By recasting the ancient conflict between history and poetry, Aeschylus enables both empathy (with the enemy) and critical distance (toward power). He asks the Athenian public to regard the stage not as a mirror to their city but as a slender ribbon binding an imagined

Sousa with a real Athens. This is not an inconsiderable task. By fictionalizing a historical event, Aeschylus seeks less to misalign reality than to
realign its connection to the aesthetic.

We see this in full force when we turn to modern playwrights. While implied in Aeschylus, the parabasis in their work is direct and self-conscious.
Their plays, of course, presuppose two centuries of aesthetic differentiation,
the emergence of art as institution. So what does parabasis look like in
modern drama?

An obvious example, Peter Weiss's "The Persecution and Assassination of Jean-Paul Marat As Performed by the Inmates of the Asylum of
Charenton Under the Direction of the Marquis de Sade" (1965), is a good
starting point. Even the title itself, long as a whip, cracks with tension between art and reality. Like Aeschylus, Weiss's play makes use of historical
personages, taking as its kernel two facts: (1) Sade was confined to a luna-
tic asylum where he staged dramas with the inmates and (2) the murder
of the revolutionary Jean-Paul Marat in his bathtub by Charlotte Cor-
day. The encounter of Sade, the libertine, and Marat, the man of action,
however, is imaginary, fusing the Romantic battle between history and
art. The mad Sade serves as the director of the play about the revolution
but also appears in cameo, often engaging in political and philosophical
fights with Marat, goading him with irony.

Although not parabatic in the Aristophanic mode, the characters often
address the audience, real or insane, such as when the Herald, picking up
the chorus's cry for "revolution now," closes off the first act, saying:

We will since it's a play not actual history
Postpone it with an interval We guarantee
That after your refreshments and debating
You'll find Marat still in his bathtub waiting. (71)

Here the Herald simply winks at the audience, letting it know that he
knows that they all know this is just a play after all. Similarly, toward the
beginning, Coulmier, the director of the hospital, interrupts a dialogue
about religion, reminding Sade that "we agreed to make cuts to this passage" since in 1808, the date of the play's production, "nobody objects to
the church" (29).[3] The reference is to art making.

Unlike Aristophanes, where the curtain of make-believe is drawn back
and the chorus talks to the audience as Athenian citizens, Weiss creates
a play within a play. The difference is divergent conceptions of aesthetic

autonomy. In Aristophanes, drama—qua drama—is enmeshed in civic life, but in Weiss drama struggles for political relevance after two centuries of aesthetic compartmentalization. Whereas Aristophanes could expect a homogeneous audience, and, in fact, real people he was lambasting, Weiss faces the anonymity of multiple publics in various cities. The audience is a generalized amalgam rather than an identifiable group of people. Moreover, in Aristophanes the questions are historical: What should we do about the Peloponnesian War? Who will lead us? In Weiss, by contrast, they are philosophical: Is drama still germane to modern society? What is the relationship between art and action?

Both plays are conscious of themselves as art but claim different relationships to the public. Aristophanes can still rail against politicians, unfair judges, and gullible citizens with the hope of real-life and real-time impact upon civic life. This possibility of direct participation in the empirical world is severely limited in Weiss's play by the institution of art itself. What authority does art now have as one specialized domain to speak about matters outside its expertise? This self-knowledge yields to the irony I noted earlier (I know I am a play and I know that you know I am a play), a trope that shortens the distance between play and spectators. Both are bound by this secret. Irony, normally a distancing technique, actually brings play and spectators closer together.

The parabasis is transformed into a thematic from a structural operation. That is to say, the play between illusion and reality becomes a subject of art, part of its postmodern self-consciousness, where the work talks about itself as art. For instance, the two protagonists incorporate the struggle between writing and acting. The decadent Sade mocks Marat, who is taking notes in his bathtub. Give up, he tells him. "You said yourself / nothing can be achieved by scribbling / Long ago I abandoned my masterpiece" (82). But Marat responds that he wanted to merge the two in his own life. "When I wrote / I always wrote with action in mind" (82). Writing was a preparation for the great deed. Ironically, he dies not leading the revolution but composing, exactly as he is portrayed in David's familiar portrait. The stage directions explicitly have him holding his pen with his right hand and his papers with his left, with his head drooping over the tub.

In the epilogue, however, Marat climbs out of his tub, as Coulmier, the director of the hospital, comes forward, addressing the audience, members of Parisian exclusive circles that attended Sade's performances. Closing "the history book" and returning to 1808, he reassures them with talk of the social progress that has been made since the revolution. "For today we live in far different times / We have no oppressors, no violent times." But as Coulmier congratulates Sade for his triumph, the patients come rushing forward to the rising din of the music, shouting "Charenton Charenton / Napoleon Napoleon / Nation Nation / Revolution Revolution / Copulation Copulation" (101). A struggle ensues, with the nurses striking the inmates with batons. In the ongoing melee, Coulmier gives the signal for the curtain. What was supposed to provide light entertainment for the Parisian elites turns into a political uprising. Art can have real consequences—on the stage—inciting the inmates with revolutionary zeal.

It is ironic that Coulmier, who originally wanted to rehabilitate patients aesthetically—"we prefer therapy through education especially art" (4)—realizes that the play itself led to the uprising of the inmates. No longer able to control the rebellion, he can only end it by dropping the curtain of make-believe, to pretend that it did not happen. But can he do it? Are the "enlightened ladies and pious gentlemen" confident that the upheaval won't spill out from the stage to the spectator galleries, from the asylum to the city, from insanity to sanity? Are they safe in their categories? For insurgents have a way of jumping from the barricades to the stage.

Despite the questions of art's relevance, art can lead to action. But this action is limited within the represented play, within the confines of art itself. Can art spill onto politics and politics onto art? Weiss's play seems to answer affirmatively, yet also tentatively because its self-knowledge tugs at it tirelessly. Weiss looks for artistic efficacy that Aristophanes presumed. He has no choice but to stage his parabasis as a play within a play.

As does Günter Grass in "The Plebeians Rehearse the Uprising. A German Tragedy." A parabasis in reverse occurs when striking workers occupy the stage, demanding the attention and help of the director. Blending history and fiction, Grass takes the real events of the workers' strike of June 17, 1953, in East Berlin to examine that interplay between action and performance. For while the uprisings are taking place on the streets, Brecht is directing his adaptation of Shakespeare's "Coriolanus."[4] But the strikers burst onto the stage, asking the renowned director to lend cultural clout to their demands for greater justice and freedom. In so doing, they place the socialist playwright in a terrible dilemma: Is he going to support the workers in their justifiable pursuit of their rights? Or will he uphold the state that underwrites his artistic projects? And if he does the latter, what type of cultural autonomy would he have? If he espouses his own dramatical technique of estrangement (*Entfremdung*), how can he himself find the requisite purchase from which to evaluate society?

Grass props these questions, however, on top of a more fundamental issue: the difference between reality and art. For, as Brecht is staging "Coriolanus," reality intervenes upon him, forcing him to rethink his art and the revolution. Is art, a committed practice at that, responsible for events and to people outside its domain? Is Brecht, in other words, trapped as the subject of his own play? Brecht, named as the Boss, shouts at his assistants to "get these amateurs out of my theater." But the foreman counters: "we don't know how to act in a theater.—But we want to be in the way." Then all the workers cry out: "We demand freedom!" (Grass 1966: 66–67). The plasterer reminds the Boss that the government is building him a new theater (32). And the Boss himself wonders how he can forget the state that feeds him. The truth is concrete, he says, but "this is a rehearsal." One of the characters shouts out "What is a rehearsal when the toiling masses, / Ignoring their directors, start acting on their own?" (59).

As in Weiss, we have here a play about a play but also a dramatization of the limits of aesthetic autonomy. Can art afford to live within its own confines, to stage the gap between itself and society? Can Brecht continue with his play when striking workers break onto his set? Like Weiss and Aristophanes, Grass dramatizes the conflict between reality and semblance. But unlike Aristophanes, he resorts to the Brechtian concept of alienation as a way of addressing this tension. Since art can longer step out of itself, as in the ancient parabasis, it tries to crack the audience's identification with the stage. By superimposing one rebellion over the other, it asks the question: Which uprising is more real? The one in Shakespeare, the one on Brecht's stage, or the one on the streets of East Berlin in the summer of 1953? This motif runs through the whole play. One of the characters, Volumnia (Coriolanus's mother,) asks the Boss what would happen if they were not in Rome or in London, but in East Berlin, and "our people come storming onto the stage" (18). The hairdresser brings this point home, inviting the Boss to put on a real play in the streets, in front of the tanks:

Come on, Boss. Come, and crawl out of the shell:
And we'll put on a play for the whole world,
Enacted in the street, on barricades. (92)

While the Boss wants to use the workers to stage the uprisings for his play, they shout for liberty. Whereas he alludes to Shakespeare and the Roman historian Livy (one of Shakespeare's sources), they cite Brecht and Marx. Although in Brecht's play the plebeians are victorious, in real life they are crushed by the tanks.[5]

Aristophanes demonstrated the value of art by showing *in the parabasis* that art is just discourse, that it can claim truth-value for its statements in the public sphere. At that moment, he punctured art's status, as maker of semblance, to identify with the audience. The modern playwright does the opposite. Using the trope of alienation, he interferes with the audience's embrace of the characters. In epic theater, Brecht wrote, there must be "no illusion that the player is identical with the characters and the performance with the play" (1957: 195). In part, this entailed turning an object the audience is aware of "into something peculiar, striking, and unexpected" (143). These techniques, having to do with stagecraft, can be witnessed on the stage only. Brecht, for instance, referred to the method Chinese actors used to express awareness of being watched by the audience in order to frustrate the latter's fantasy of being unseen (91).

By use of these techniques, Grass achieves dramatic remoteness through endless self-reference. If Aristophanes' didacticism was immediate, here it is indirect: Grass writing about Brecht's staging of Shakespeare's "Coriolanus" that itself dealt with actual uprisings. The intervention of the workers, both historically real and aesthetically staged, suspends disbelief by showing that art could never be a thing in itself. The audience is hit throughout with the message that art cannot exist within the "House of Culture" (Grass 1966: 58). The play is primarily fabricated. This is its paradox: the play pretends to be unreal, all the while claiming to be based on reality.

Yet "he who confronts the paradoxical exposes himself to reality," Friedrich Dürrenmatt writes in his 1964 wild play, *The Physicists*. Dürrenmatt tries to unravel this tension between the real and the actual by looking at the conflict between sanity and insanity. His work concerns three scientists: Johann Wilhelm Möbius (the world's greatest living physicist), a man who claims to be Newton and another, who believes he is Einstein, are all housed in the sanatorium run by the diabolical psychiatrist, Mathilde van Zahnd. Playing with the madness-sanity duality, the play forces the audience to think about the borders that make up their own world. "Drama can dupe the spectator into exposing himself to reality, but cannot compel him to withstand it or even to master it" (96). Mastering this reality would, of course, be impossible if we don't know who is sane and who is not, where art begins and where it ends.

Art, Dürrenmatt suggests, more than any other medium, forces people to confront social contradictions in a space beyond logic and proof. At the end of the play we are not sure if protagonists are mad pretending to be scientists or the other way around, or, for that matter, if the audience is foolish for putting up with the antics. If we are not certain, it is because the drama itself no longer knows if the world is a stage or vice versa. Aristophanes had no such doubts. The real folly was the war rather than what was presented on stage. The parabasis, after all, was not a play within a play but a moment of unmediated political discourse within the space opened up by drama. Modern works, by contrast, can't seek real-life impact. By exploring the interplay of fabrication and verity, they argue that we come to truth through fiction, even if we don't know what that truth is.

When the Countess Madeleine in Richard Strauss's opera, *Capriccio* (1942), cannot choose between her two suitors, the composer, Flamand, and the poet, Olivier, she accepts her brother's suggestion that they all perform an opera about themselves. So she stages one in the theater of her rococo chateau outside Paris. "Today's events, as we have lived them—write and compose them as an opera" (203). The poet and the composer, representing poetry and music, struggle for Madeleine's heart. What takes precedence, poetry, music, or theater itself? "We are already in the middle of the discussion on the basic argument of our time," the count says as the poet and composer argue over the hierarchy of the arts. The servants, who come to prepare the salon for dinner, are bemused by the events, scoffing at the idea that nowadays "everyone plays the theater." They cannot be fooled, however, as they know that the count wants to have a tryst with the lead actress, Clairon, while the countess does not know whom to select as her lover. "And to make up her mind she lets them write her an opera," says one servant. "How can you learn from an opera?" asks another (217).

Perhaps we learn nothing concrete. But the opera enacts that strange dance between objectivity and illusion. The countess herself does distinguish between what is real and what is fake. She neither wants to choose between music and poetry, seeing opera as a synthesis of both, nor does she want to decide between fantasy and reality, recognizing that life is a fusion of both. This is why in the fugue treating the theme "words or music," she responds to Flamand's rejection of theater as trickery, by arguing that it is not a deception at all. "The stage unveils the secret of reality. We see ourselves in a magic mirror. Theater is the affecting symbol of life" (139). We learn about ourselves by turning over the veil. The countess seeks self-knowledge by fictionalizing reality. The point of her own play is to maintain this indecisiveness. "When we, in our world of illusion," the actress, Clairon, says, "come too close to reality, Art is in danger of burning its wings" (85).

When semblance and truth blend into one another art loses its ability to offer counterstatements. Clairon understands the circular game art plays: It needs leeway to survive and it survives by offering leeway. This is the parabasis in modern theater, the capacity to mediate between acting and the real thing.[6]

Framed Narratives

The theater, as I have stated earlier, with its live performances and the unmediated presence of the audience dramatizes this interpenetration of illusion and fact. Can works of fiction manage the same type of parabatic digression, when the reader holds a book in front of her, a work that seems silent and dead?

The 1937 short story, "In Dreams Begin Responsibilities," by the American poet and writer Delmore Schwartz takes on this dialectic, in this case, the crisscrossing of life and film, reverie and actuality. We find our unnamed narrator, a young man of twenty-one, in the cinema watching a movie of his parents' courtship. This direct intervention into life by art forces the narrator to confront some sad truths about his family.

Schwartz achieves his parabasis by crossing into another art. He defamiliarizes, so to speak, the narrator's life by incorporating into prose film's claim at greater verisimilitude. So we have then a melding of two arts, moving pictures with static words. By introducing an alien medium into the reading process, Schwartz brings to the fore the conflict between real and reel. For the protagonist is watching a movie of his life rather than a plot hatched by a screenwriter. Yet, the remoteness brought about by a new medium allows the reader more immediate access into the mind of the young man. As his father picks up his fiancée and as they enter the booth of a fortune-teller at Coney Island, the narrator begins to sense the unfolding of a personal tragedy. We get truth via the distancing effect of art.

As we watch the narrator watching his life, we suspect that the relationship will sour. We get a sense of his sorrow early on when the projector malfunctions: "I am awakened to myself and my unhappiness just as my interest was rising" (1978: 3). As the projector resumes, the narrator detects disquiet in his father and he himself stirs "uneasily" in his chair. Recognizing his father's peremptory treatment of his fiancée, the narrator begins to whimper, which elicits the irritated look from the old lady next to him. "There, there, all of this is only a movie, young man, only a movie" (5). By now the father's harsh character becomes apparent, as does the mother's demurring nature. When he proposes to her in the restaurant, the son screams out "Don't do it. It's not too late to change your minds, both of you. Nothing good will come of it, only remorse, hatred, scandal, and two children whose characters are monstrous" (6). Here a member of the (fictitious) audience, in a reverse parabasis, cries at the screen, reality trying to influence art, because art itself has intervened on reality. The usher runs down and the old lady again scolds him. But the narrator can't control himself, anxious at his inability to edit the action. Finally an argument erupts in the tent of a fortune-teller, his mother wishing to stay while his father storms out. The son shouts out again to both of them only to be dragged out by the usher. At the end, the narrator wakes up from his nightmare. It was not a film after all. And we realize that this vision was like the idea in the Platonic cave, an illusion of a representation of a life, flickering images of an unhappy family.

Although the young man knows he is watching a film, he cannot, like the other viewers, separate himself from it completely. He seeks active involvement in the movie's unfolding plot as he comes face to face with the ensuing catastrophe. When he yells to the protagonists on the screen, begging them to rethink their decision to marry, he wants to have an impact on his family via art. Is his life a film or is the film his life? What is imitating what? Was the incident all a nightmare? Did he wake up in the morning to the bleak winter of his twenty-first birthday or had he fallen asleep in the cinema?

Yet the story says that art is genuine because it prods us to change our lives. Even though art occupies a separate dimension on the screen, it allows us to imagine what we are otherwise unwilling or incapable of doing, in this case, of confronting the dissolution of a family—much like Cheever's "The Swimmer." In the realm of art we come to terms with veiled truths.

Schwartz achieves a parabasis on the protagonist by forcing him to reconsider how the world of dreams intersects the world of experience. By assimilating film into his narrative, Schwartz also accomplishes a formal parabasis on readers, compelling them to think about the differences not only between fiction and experience but also between prose and film.

Stéphane Mallarmé had attempted this forty years before Schwartz in his path-breaking poem "Un coup de dés" ("A Throw of the Dice," 1897). The poem reflects on the cinematographic possibilities of poetry, showing one more time the dual character of art and the overlap between aesthetic and ordinary experience. Indeed, "Un coup de dés" brings to poetry the challenges and lessons of cinema, becoming one of the first literary texts to conduct a dialogue between cinematography and poetics (Wall-Romana 2005). Moreover, Mallarmé strived to synthesize different forms of art, in his case music. His pursuits, he wrote in the preface to the poem, "are joined under a strange influence, that of Music, as it is heard at a concert; several of its methods, which seemed to me to apply to Literature, are to be found here" (Mallarmé 1994:123). The result is a revolutionary and scandalous attempt to defy typographic laws. The parabatic here then involves the poet's attempt to break out of the constraints of print by embracing the formal qualities of other media.

Thematically, if one could use this word for Mallarmé's text, the poem deals with chance. It ruminates on and tries to recreate the idea of contingency expressed in the title, the act of throwing dice. But it does so formally above all. For what is visually striking about the poem is its physical layout, which, as Mallarmé notes, participates in two pursuits at the same time, free verse and prose poetry, another crossing of literary boundaries (1994: 123). Like an ancient inscription, it has no punctuation marks to guide the reader; but unlike these documents, compressed together without any gaps, it expands out like the universe, giving as much meaning to spaces as to letters. As the helmsman works to maneuver the ship between chance and waves, the reader attempts to steer among the words without the benefit of syntax, traveling without a map, so to speak. They are desperate for the "line" in Moses's poem. Ship and reader are tossed by the unforeseen.

Reading the text is a challenge because it is written in four different type sizes. The title, in the largest font, highlighted in bold and capitalized, serves as the leitmotif of the text. But rather than coming into view in the first page, it scatters over the poem's sixteen pages: "Un coup de dés jamais n'abolira le hazard"(A throw of the dice will never abolish chance). Other narratives in different font sizes are dispersed throughout the poem, overlapping one another. For example, immediately after the line, "A Throw of the Dice Will Never" (Un coup de dés jamais), there appears in capitalized smaller font the following, "Even when launched in eternal circumstances from the depths of a shipwreck" (126). Readers have to map out the flow of these two currents of words along with two others without the benefit of syntax, grammar, and punctuation. At times readers are not sure whether they should read left to right or top to bottom, as both directions make sense (130). They have to provide both the map and the code by which to read it at the same time, an extreme example, no doubt, of the way literature works, fashioning new languages with which we interpret it.[7]

When shown the poem by Mallarmé, Paul Valéry was struck by its "unprecedented arrangement." He felt that he was looking at the "form and pattern of thought, placed for the first time in finite space." Space, expectancy, and cognition were given a temporal manifestation. He wondered finally whether he had not just witnessed "the enactment of the Creation of Language" (1972: 309–310). By this he meant that Mallarmé was privileging writing, as opposed to the author, in the act of poetic communication. "Mallarmé was doubtless the first to see and to foresee in its full extent the necessity to substitute language itself for the person who until then had been supposed to be its owner" (Barthes 1977: 143).

Nothing that hypertext creates today could be as shocking and awesome as "Un coup de dés" because it already anticipates hypertext's quasi-authorless, readerly prose. Diving through the poem is like the ride the man and the woman take through the abstract terrain of Welty's "No Place for You, My Love," a protean landscape of azure mists and waving heat. Like the couple returning safely from their descent to the south, readers stepping out from Mallarmé's text feel the jolt between contingency and predictability that we saw also in Aristophanes. The genius of Mallarmé's poem lies in demonstrating this with minimum content, relying on signs themselves to communicate that disjuncture between literary signification and actuality. He enacts that interplay of fact and fable by reinterpreting it as a tension between form and content, cinematography and poetry, words and signs.

Unlike Mallarmé, Schwartz relies less on form than on theme to accomplish this, showing the overlap of dreams and art. Both have the potential to free us from the denotative load of language, from the rigor of logical thinking, from the requirement of consistency. Images are released from their meaning, giving us much latitude in our expression and thinking. Art is in a sense nothing but a leeway from life. Neither escape from being, nor the reverse of work, it is a flexible understanding of rules. If art ends up drawing margins around life, it is because freedom resides along margins. But Schwartz's narrator, like Mallarmé's, poses neither dreams nor film as the opposite of reality, showing, rather, a reciprocal give-and-take. Far from fading into either slumber or a celluloid fantasy, he faces his life with cruel realism. But it is hard for him to reflect on his being without the prism of art: Life takes aesthetic shape; signs point to images; dreams become tangible.

By fictionalizing reality we come to truth. This is why the Portuguese author, Fernando Pessoa (1888–1935), says that "the poet is a faker." In fact, "he even fakes he's suffering / The pain he's really feeling." His audience, as a consequence, reads about a pain that is "completely fictional" (1986: 167). The ache becomes a representation of a once tangible feeling, one now conjured up, made distant by the pull of words and images. This remoteness is a product of what I have been calling parabasis, the margin of deviation where we begin to think about truth and fancy. "They say I fake or lie / In everything I write," writes Pessoa in "This." Composing and dreaming is like standing on a terrace, he says, "facing something else." It is casting one's eyes on objects far away, communicating with things not readily at hand (1986: 168).[8]

This divergence is not only ethical, the gap between truth and fakery, but also formal, the jump from one medium to another. Not having at his disposal the public's encounter with the dramatic spectacle that theater (and to a certain extent film) can expect, the poet or prose writer brings about parabasis by incorporating other art forms. The simultaneous alienation and empathy that Aristophanes attained by accosting the audience directly, Schwartz's prose achieves by embracing the properties of cinematography. Fearing film's rise as the dominant aesthetic medium of the twentieth century (his story was published in 1937), he responds by adopting film's parabatic strategies.

The Greek writer, Alki Zei, rises to this challenge with postmodern virtuosity. Her 1991 novel, *Achilles' Fiancée*, comes as close as possible to the verisimilitude of a movie that prose can attain. Like Schwartz's narrator, Eleni/Daphne sees herself as stepping in and out of a film screen, converting day-to-day experience into images, passing between gestalt and aesthetic creation. This theme is structurally built into the novel itself, fusing content and form again. Written as two separate narrations, one taking place during the German occupation of Greece and the subsequent Greek Civil War, the other on a film set in Paris during the uprisings of 1968, the novel takes on the struggle between art and life both in a figurative and literal sense. The heroine does not know what is tangible and what is imaginary, whether she is an autonomous woman or an actor following the instructions of the director or her husband. The aesthetic/realist disjunction in her life is structurally mirrored in the ongoing switch between present and past.[9]

At the end, the two narratives, until then running independently, fuse together into real time. In the present the actors, "set free" by the director, say goodbye to one another. But in the past Daphne, who has finally returned to Greece with her daughter, is awoken by her mother on April 21, 1967 with cries of "Dictatorship" (356–57). Having finally settled in Greece, Daphne is forced to flee again to Paris where she takes up the role of an extra in the sentimental film. Past and present crash into each other like two locomotives. Which is the real "horror train"? The one on the set, the dictatorship, or the entirety of Daphne's life that took her from a local station in Athens, to Rome, Paris, Moscow, all the way to Tashkent, then back to Athens, to end up on a movie in Paris? "*The Horror Train* is beginning. Trains keep chasing Eleni in her life. Real and fake ones" (62).

In this interaction between the real and the fake, Zei accomplishes her parabasis by deftly switching between past and present, film and novel, first and third narration. We get to know her life through flashbacks to Daphne's (her nom de guerre) original involvement in the resistance against the Germans, her attachment to the guerilla leader, Achilles, his escape to the mountains and eventually to the Soviet Union, her imprisonment and her release, and her two-year quest for Achilles, eventually reuniting with him half way around the world in Tashkent. The transition between Eleni and Daphne, movie set and real life, however, is achieved with the techniques of the cinema: "'The Horror Train' scene—take—frame" at the beginning of the scene and "cut" at the end. We "hear" the clacker with each change of scene, which could last one paragraph or a couple of pages. Zei borrows these cinematographic properties in order to blur the edge between aesthetic modes and between fact and fiction. For we are not really certain, when the clacker falls, whether we are in the past or the present.

For instance, in the movie set the carriage rocks suddenly as Eleni looks at Stefanos and Panos who are about to jump off the train. But after the "cut" Eleni remembers how Panos had to leap off a real train during the German occupation. Similarly, when a young woman is at the train station about to leave, the narration shows Daphne leaving Rome on her way to Paris (1991: 122). While in Paris a French woman, Genevieve, tells Eleni that she could put her in touch with a French director who could make a film out of her greater-than-life-tale (289). In a reflexive moment, Eleni wonders why she ever thought life resembled acting, changing roles, leaving one scene for another. One day slipping into the editing room, Eleni observes how the assistant director works with the frames. Imagining her life as a reel of film, she wonders which episodes she would emphasize and which she would gloss over (317).

Thus Zei's work treats the cinema as both theme and structuring device, imagining the power of film through fiction. In crossing back and forth between prose and film, it breaches art's borders, creating the esthetic clearance that Aristophanes perfected in the parabasis. Without a chorus to remove their masks and hurl their insults at the crowd, the novelist confuses the readers, so to speak, making them believe that they are watching a movie. She then draws an explicit comparison between the fakery in novel/movie making and the fakery in life, between fiction in art and lies in a marriage.

Zei's novel takes to heart the lesson of Schwartz's story, namely that we learn by fictionalizing our life. Daphne realizes that she has been subservient to Achilles and to Stalin after she projects her life as a screenplay. Only when she serves as an extra in the French production does she discover her own secondary role in life. Although she, like Schwartz's young man, cannot edit her life, she resolves to gain agency. While she lets the past (mistakes, illusions, idealizations, and contingencies) run its course, she begins to reflect on her future as a new person in the realm of invention. The distancing of art enables her to examine herself as a disembodied person with two identities. Art allows her to envision autonomy, her independence from domineering men and powerful institutions.

Her schizophrenia of self-identification, does not lead, as one might expect, to madness but rather to self-knowledge. By projecting her split personalities and divided loyalties onto the screen, she finds direction. In other words, aesthetic autonomy allows her to imagine personal autonomy. Art becomes an arena for simulation, for inventing new possibilities, as Richard Wright had discovered. Eleni/Daphne is a faker—like the novelist and the director—because she knows the importance of semblance to discovering truth.

The postmodern writer, like Zei, achieves her parabasis by crossing into another art, and from there gaining the distance to reflect on history. How can realist fiction achieve this aesthetic digression? We can examine this question by turning to a Greek short story, "Moskóv-Selím," (1988) by Georgios Vizyenos (1849–96). Unaffected by avant-garde textual theories, this text seems at first reading a slice of life. Yet it begins by drawing a parallel between aesthetic and personal autonomy. The text deals with Moskóv-Selím, who, as his name suggests, straddles the edge of sexual, ethnic, religious, and national existence a century before Eleni/Daphne. For, although born a Muslim subject of the Ottoman Empire, he comes to identify himself as Russian. Having been rejected by his father and by the Ottoman state, he finds acceptance at the hands of his Russian captors whom he has fought as a Turkish soldier in the Balkans. When the Greek narrator discovers him, he lives as a hermit in a house resembling a Russian cottage, dressed in Russian clothes. The narrator is so taken by Moskóv-Selím's biographical and architectural bricolage that he resolves to write about him.

In a two-paragraph prologue unrelated at all to the realist narrative that follows, the narrator directs himself to Moskóv-Selím and also his audience. "I don't doubt," he writes, "that the fanatics of your race will curse the memory of a 'believer' because he opened the sanctuary of his heart to the unholy eyes of an infidel." He also fears that "the fanatics of my own race will reproach a Greek author because he did not conceal your virtue, or did not substitute a Christian hero in his account" (1988: 187). This introductory section, separated physically by a double space and three stars from the main narrative, is not essential to the plot. Its purpose is to highlight the relationship of the word to the world, literature and national/religious identities. But it is not meant as a playful, self-reflexive allusion so typical of postmodernist writing. Although Vizyenos lived in the latter part of the nineteenth century, he was engaged in what the Greeks called "ithografia," usually translated as folkloric realism.

Yet, even he, steeped in this traditional genre, can't help but address that gap of parabatic possibility, which, as in Mallarmé, is set off typographically rather than metaphorically. Moskóv-Selím's marginal life moves the author to open a place on the page, to give shape to him, to rescue him from death's oblivion. Moskóv-Selím, the character, comes to be in that writerly interval between the author's parabatic address to his audience and the narration that follows. In so doing, he brings about aesthetic empathy in his readers—the compassionate portrayal of the "inexorable enemy of my nation"—and distances them from reality—by underscoring the limits of identity formation.

Indeed, Moskóv-Selím's crossing of national and religious borders is prefigured in his childhood by his violation of the laws of gender. Raised by his mother in the harem until he was twelve, he acquires "gentle" and "peaceable" qualities as well as a "vulnerable" heart. His father dismisses him as a sissy with his long hair, even though, as a young man, he shows valor in war. But this crucial experience with femininity, literally an enclave within the larger masculine society (paralleling the empathetic space of literature in the clamor of nationalism), allows Selím later on to fashion a separate world for himself. Like an artist, he fabricates his own retreat, part reality part fiction. "Selím had constructed for himself a Russian life in that Hellenic land because his *lively imagination . . .* filled in the gaps in that life so that what for the rest of us was comic and ridiculous disappeared from before his eyes in the same way that that good 'hanúmissa' [his mother] had created through her own imagining a girl child by dressing and making up the extremely manly Selím as a daughter" (225, my emphasis).

The narrator's observations about the affect of Moskóv-Selím's up-bringing on his psychological development illuminate the parabatic nature of the author's craft. Literature invents a world that is different from but not opposite of the ordinary one. Vizyenos never says that fiction and reality are feuding rivals. Indeed, he highlights other domains, such as the harem, where the imagination blossoms. But he is interested in this interplay between the fictive and the real, in demonstrating what happens when biography is transposed into signs. He wants, in other words, to examine the parallel between Moskóv-Selím's invented Russian steppe and the author's own recasting of Moskóv-Selím as a subject for art. For both thrive on breaking and maintaining fences.

Vizyenos insists on the importance of these borders even as his protagonist transgresses them all his life. Moskóv-Selím's nobility and wisdom stem from his inbetweenness rather than from his bravery in war—from his courage literally to embody the Other. He constitutes what Victor Turner would call "liminal" figures, people who are "betwixt and between," neither here nor there (1969: 95). The state of liminality, he explains, is a "period of interstructural situation," a transition from one realm to another, say from adolescence to adulthood (1967: 93). In this condition of ambiguity the neophytes are neither boys nor men, inhabiting a stage that resembles neither past nor future.

Turner's insights on rites of passage shed light here on parabasis as a structural contradiction between semblance and reality. Freed from laws of the universe and the mores of society, parabasis signifies a channel of pent-up promise. Moskóv-Selím thrives in this literary realm of ambiguity both as character and man. For his life is parabatic, a deliberate confusion of custom and category. But when this passage of paradox collapses, he dies. Unable to bear the thought that the Russians are about to invade the Ottoman Empire, Selím takes his last breath in the presence of the author. Parabasis can no longer maintain the tension between actuality and illusion.

Vizyenos suggests that parabasis is the ambiguous zone of inbetweenness staving off the pressures of empiricism. It is a magic place where a Turk lives like a Russian and where a Greek author saves him from oblivion. The salvation, of course, is aesthetic. Whereas Moskóv-Selím dies, he is resurrected in literature. This poetic strategy is as old as the Epic of Gilgamesh and the odes of Pindar. Yet Vizyenos reworks the traditional elegy. On the one hand, his story makes readers empathize with the deceased friend; they long for compensation in the aesthetic realm. Yet when they discover that Moskóv-Selím has been resurrected in fiction, they are alienated from him. They grasp and lose him the moment he turns into a literary character. The act of fictionalization brings about sympathy and distance. It is restorative and depleting.

The narrator in Orhan Pamuk's *Snow* (2004) discovers this too in his quest for aesthetic deliverance. A fiction writer himself, he is portrayed very much like the author, Orhan Pamuk, writing a novel called "Snow." Here the postmodern novel, contrary to poststructuralist convention, asks us to see the narrator and author as one and the same person. The author, narrator, and Ka are writers, reflecting on their craft. The narrator tries to recreate the life of his dead friend, Ka, a poet and writer of a volume of poems that are informed by the crystalline shape of snowflakes. Cast as a political thriller and set against the conflict between secularism and Islamism in Turkey, the novel ponders the push and pull between experience and art, untreated life and its aesthetic re-enactment.[10] As the narrator attempts with his art to bring to life his dead friend, he visits the frontier city of Kars four years later, a place torn by religious upheaval. As he wanders its snowy streets, the narrator becomes Ka, retracing his route, entering the same café, being met by the same charcoal-colored dog, and falling in love with the same woman, the beautiful Ipek. "There had been many moments when I almost felt I *was* Ka" (411).

While he tries to restore Ka, he searches for the deep mystery of his poems, which were arranged along the "six-pronged snowflake's nineteen points," and which were taken by the assassin after he had murdered Ka (376). Biographical recreation goes along with literary reconstruction. Unable to find the lost book of poetry, the narrator then proceeds to write the novel about Ka in Kars. What we have here is not aesthetic transcendence, since the volume of poems seems to have vanished forever, but the creation of something new. Ka lives on but as a fictional figure, a something else, so to speak, because novels, the narrator realizes, cannot give back the prototype. They can only talk about the difference the footprints Ka leaves on the snowy roads of Kars and his desire to behold them before they melt.

The narrator says as much to Fazil, the Islamist who marries Ipek's sister, Kadife. Having learned that the renowned Istanbul author was planning to write a book about the people of Kars, Fazil is certain that Western readers would come to interpret them in a binary conflict of East and West that they love so much, a clash of civilizations or as examples of modernizing societies: "If you write a book set in Kars and put me in it, I'd like to tell your readers not to believe anything you say about me, anything you say about any of us. No one could understand us from so far away" (2004: 426). Fazil is anxious about the power of art to misalign, fearing that Western readers, secure in their "superior" humanism, would hold the Turkish provincials as "sweet and funny." But the narrator contradicts him,—"No one believes in that way what he reads in a novel" (426)—confident that he has raised numerous postmodern flags to prevent such facile identifications. That is to say, the "sentimental" narrator/author believes that he has included enough tropes—irony, self-reference, novel-within-a-novel—that no one would read it biographically. The refraction created around the novel by the postmodern mirrors discourage Western readers from seeing the text as a reflection of real people and places.

This refraction—what I have elsewhere called aesthetic leeway—is the space in "The Persians" between the stage and the audience, which separates and unites them. The parabasis in Aeschylus was the air between the actual ruins on the acropolis and the theatrical reconstruction of the purveyors of that destruction. Aristophanes converted this gap into a metaphor for artistic engagement, a way of understanding art as keeper and violator of illusions. The parabasis then is not a thing or an object but an energeia, a dynamic that literature puts into effect.

This dynamic means that the novel (*Snow* and "Snow") can offer neither the mimetic realism that Fazil seeks nor the aesthetic redemption that Ka aspired to. It is a mystery like the cryptic poem composed by Ka. In writing Ka's story, the novelist (both the real and imaginary Orhan Pamuk) eulogizes Ka's daring to compose verses in the midst of political turmoil and personal despair. The secret crystalline shape inspiring Ka's texts, that enigmatic accord he craves, is not some Sufi mystery or philosophical conundrum but rather the parabatic fringe (like the frontier city of Kars itself)—the periphery where reality and reconstruction touch.

Thus two types of snow illuminate the novel: the actual snowflakes falling in Kars and the "imaginary" snowflake containing the secrets of poetry. In the liquid space between them are dreams. "It snows only once in our dreams" Ka had once written (4). This is the region of "reverie," into which Ka fell during his original drive to Kars, a domain of "optimism," a netherland of inbetweenness—Welty's "south of the south," Cheever's river of interconnected swimming pools, Vizyenos's reconstructed Russian steppe, and Pessoa's "neither dream nor not dream" but "unwake without end." It is the region of potential and aspiration without which reality would make no sense.

This is the whole point of liminality, perhaps. We cannot really know the actual if we cannot compare it with its imaginary reinvention. The prompter, Monsieur Taupe, in Strauss's *Capriccio* (1942) understands this as he stumbles onto the stage. Forgotten by the others because he had fallen asleep while whispering the lines, he had just woken up as the majordomo was preparing the salon for dinner. Monsieur Taupe spends his life underground as the "invisible ruler of a magical world" (223). Pleased to meet him, the majordomo welcomes his unexpected guest "to the real world" (225). Only temporarily, the prompter says, for when he sits in his box, he sets the whole world in motion, making the "great wheel of the theater" turn:

The deep thoughts of our poets, I whisper them
softly to myself—and everything starts to live.
Reality is mirrored in front of me like uncanny phantoms.
My own whispering lulls me to sleep.
If I sleep, I become an event!
The actors cease to speak—the public wakes up! (227)

The prompter makes the author's apparitions appear on the stage but the more he whispers the more he is in danger of falling asleep, thereby ruining the whole spell. This then is the moment of parabasis when the chorus pinches us and we become confused, not knowing if we are looking at a play or at ourselves.

This is fine, some would say. But opera, plays, the novel, even movies are part of old art—a tradition of narrative. Parabasis, they argue, depends on stories. Does it have a place in the paratactic universe of the computer database that accumulates lists of information without making distinctions among them? Can literary works compete with the interactive, colorful, watery texts created by the computer? Is there a place for the aesthetic experience in digital utopia?

§6 The Future of a Fiction

Or, Is There a Parabatic in the Paratactic?

"The age demanded . . . a prose kinema."
——Ezra Pound, "H. S. Mauberley"

Are we back to where we started? At the end of the book? The unceasing accumulation of data in the computer age seems to shift our focus away from narrative to the nondiscriminating collection of information. We are surrounded by items, not necessarily bound in cause-and-effect relations, floating in a bay of unordered, "unsequential" data. Therefore, it would be more accurate to speak today of the "datafication" rather than the aestheticization of life.

This relational, ever-expanding universe of database challenges the significance of the story as metaphor and mode of communication in social life. Lev Manovich goes so far as to argue that "after the novel, and subsequently cinema, privileged narrative as the key form of cultural expression of the modern age, the computer age introduces its correlate—the database. Many new media objects do not tell stories." In order to come to terms with this development, he calls for a "poetics, aesthetics, and ethics of the database" (2001: 218–19).[1]

Examined closely, Manovich's announcement turns out to be a version of the death-of-art thesis, which begs the question: What implications does the disappearance of narrative have for literature? I wish to examine this question by first looking at a novel that raised it as early as 1984. *Dictionary of the Khazars: A Lexicon Novel*, the controversial book by the Serbian writer, Milorad Pavić, actually presents itself as data. This work approximates, as much as a printed text can, the seemingly random, unordered world of informational overflow. Written as a series of encyclopedic entries, it seems to resemble Flaubert's *Dictionary of Received Ideas*, the unfinished second half of *Bouvard and Pécuchet*. Yet, it also points forward to the nonlinear direction of Internet communication. Pavić exploits the multireferential nature of both traditional encyclopedia and computer database to create a nonconsecutive "story." Here we have form as content, parataxis as both theme and way of reading.

The title itself identifies the novel as a lexicon, which, à la manière de Borges, purports to be "a dictionary of the dictionaries of the Khazar question." Like Pamuk's *Snow*, it claims to be based on a vanished book. According to the preliminary notes, it reenacts a volume, *Lexicon Cosri*, printed by a Pole, Joannes Daubmannus, in 1691 that dealt with the Khazar people, an actual nation, living in the Caucasus region between the seventh and tenth centuries.

Pavić's "narrator" professes to recreate this missing book. While Pamuk's narrator reconstructs a collection of poetry inspired by the crystalline shape of snowflakes, Pavićs wants to retrieve an Ur-book. There is much postmodern irony here in so far as the novel that aspires to transcend narrative ends up celebrating it. We have books and more books, with no end in sight.

How does the novel strive to imitate the world of the database? First, like hypertext stories I explore below, it promises to free readers from the strictures of linear reading. For instance, the cover and the title page both taunt with the remark: "This book contains the FEMALE EDITION of the Dictionary. The MALE edition is almost identical. But NOT quite. Be warned that ONE PARAGRAPH is crucially different. The choice is yours." Significantly the word *choice* pops out. For in addition to selecting between the male and female versions of the text, the reader has several ways to peruse the book. He may go from beginning to end. Or she may browse through the various entries that are organized into three sections, Christian, Moslem, and Jewish, a tripartite arrangement corresponding to the three languages (Greek, Arabic, and Hebrew) of the seventeenth-century edition. Thus Pavić markets his work as an "open book," which can be added to by "new writers, compilers, and continuers" (Pavić 1989: 11). Not a palimpsest of the manuscript age, this work points to the populist Wikipedia-like mode of the future, where scribes supplement and complement what has already been written, without necessarily erasing previous texts. This is parataxis ad infinitum. Like theorists of hypertext, Pavić places absolute importance on the reader's freedom: "I tried to change the way of reading by increasing the role and responsibility of the reader in the process of creating a novel. I have left to them the decision about the choice of the plot and the development of the situations in the novel: where the reading will begin, and where it will end; the decision about the destiny of the main characters" (Pavić 1998: 145). Specifically this means that the reader

> can use the book as he sees fit. As with any other lexicon, some will look up a word or a name that interests them at the given moment, whereas others may look at the book as a text meant to be read it its entirety, from beginning to end, in one sitting . . . The book's pages can be turned from left to right or from right to left. (1998: 12)

Furthermore, the reader may actually go through the book diagonally, to get a cross-section of all three books, the Islamic, Hebrew, and Christian, by selecting entries identified with a small, triangle sign attached to names that appear in each section. The figures "Ateh" and "Kahgan," for instance, are present in all three books. The number of possible sequences is large. "Since reading in a different order implies reading a different story, the number of possible narratives is huge" (Hayles 1997: 804). On top of this, Pavić points to the other abstract possibilities by reminding us that, as a reconstruction of the lost dictionary originally written in Hebrew, Arabic, and Greek, the order of entries in the new edition is different because they are written in another language, in this case Serbo-Croatian, and now translated into over thirty other tongues.

But does this open space of readerly possibility erase the edge between fact and fable that the novel's additive mode implies? The quick answer seems to be yes. Parataxis engulfs the possibility of parabasis. But a closer look reveals some complexity. As an example of historical metafiction, of course, *Dictionary of the Khazars* plays with the conflicts of art and reality, history and literature, writing and death.[2] Indeed, the real/fake dichotomy is its organizing metaphor. We learn something about a vanished people from an imagined account. By fictionalizing their history, we come to their truth. If fiction presents itself as a way of knowing, Pavić makes the most extreme claim for realism, his book being the ultimate nonfiction. Yet a "lexicon novel" seems like an oxymoron, yoking together fact and fabrication, tedious lists with fanciful invention. We have a novel incorporating the "unmetaphoricity" of the database, a story that is not a story. But, as the author reminds us in his parabatic introduction, this is all an illusion, a postmodern game.

Pavić's novel actually registers two modes of parabasis—one thematic, the other formal—intertwined with the other. Because one of his topics is the book, Pavić wishes to underscore the perils of reading, the impact of book culture on real life. Significantly, one of the five hundred copies of the original *Lexicon Corsi* was printed in poison ink, which had a companion copy with a silver lock. The Inquisition had burned all of the copies except for these two that perished later, hence the necessity of Pavić's "reconstruction." The last page of the novel is a "preserved fragment" from the "introduction to the destroyed 1691 edition" in which that original author/editor warns readers about taking care in reading a toxic book. As in Umberto Eco's *The Name of the Rose*, books can kill—they have real-life consequences. Here we slide again from fiction to reality, when mere play becomes a bite yielding blood.

In the prefatory remarks of *Dictionary of the Khazars*, Pavić further underscores this danger with the image of two men, the author and reader, holding a puma on a rope equidistant from each other. If one of them approaches the other, the rope would slacken and the puma would attack. Only by pulling on the rope together can they keep the animal from each other. "This is why it is so hard for him who reads and him who writes to reach each other: between them lies a mutual thought captured on ropes that they pull in opposite directions" (1989: 14). This image of the book that threatens to eat both author and reader reinforces the reciprocal distance between them. It also represents the leeway between word and world that marks literary works, even those manifesting the nonlinear textuality of the lexicon/archive.

That Pavić's novel absorbs the paratactic features of the database points to the second, structural parabasis. In borrowing the relational techniques from computer technology, Pavić steps into different modes of textuality, like Mallarmé, Schwartz, or Zei who assimilated cinematographic techniques. Pavić too violates borders, here provocatively drawn between the novel and the thesaurus, between the book and the nonbook. In so doing, he poses some important questions about the fate of the book as a medium for storing information. In addition to wondering how we can know truth through fiction, in this case the history of the Khazar people, Pavić asks if books have a future. The fear of the book's death casts a pall on the novel (Hayles 1997).

In many ways, of course, his novel mourns the passing of the book as a particular technology.[3] Not that Pavić is the first writer to prophecy the demise of books. H. G. Wells foresaw the destruction of libraries, along with all manifestations of learning and art, in *The Time Machine*, published in 1895 (1996: 31–34).[4] More profoundly, Pavić's novel expresses an anxiety about the disappearance of print, which has come to define literature as an art form over the last three centuries. His book's lexicographic form anticipates the liquid textuality of the computer, which seems inimical to the permanence and autonomy of print. But does this mean that the human practices of performance, enactment, play, and make-believe will be submerged by electronic textuality? Will we cease to be interested in the tension between pretending and living?

Pavić would answer this negatively. It is one thing to mourn the twilight of print and quite another to grieve about the end of the aesthetic. Actually his novel ends up affirming the parabatic capacity of literature. The book, after all, saves the Khazars by recreating them in the aesthetic real, much as Vizyenos and Pamuk rescue their own individual characters from historical stupor. In this way, Pavić endorses that traditional idea of writing as an act of salvation, telling a story about a dead people. Despite its encyclopedic appearance and avant-garde élan, Pavić's tome is still an act of fiction claiming to be true, much like Balzac's *Père Goriot* (1994), the masterpiece of nineteenth-century realism.[5]

It is literature after all that gives shape to the discontinuous entries about the Khazar people. The archival lists and items about the Khazars require the organizing mind of the author and then the reader, both of whom, as Pavić stresses, are separated yet bound by a rope. They give this information a beginning, middle, and an end, even if the unity is temporary. Despite its antibibliographic ideology, *Dictionary of the Khazars* asserts the longevity of storytelling. If there is indeed a tug-of-war today between database and narrative, mirroring the push-and-pull image of author and reader in Pavić's preface, then this novel ends up confirming the power of narrative to give meaning to the stacks, rows, and columns in the archive. Or rather, it says that, in the Bouvard-and-Pécouchet world of infinitely expanding references, stories are still vital as is the distinction between fact and fable.

The End of the Book?

Pavić's conclusions may be self-serving, literature speaking optimistically about itself. Like all elegies, it profits by exploiting death, in this case its own. Yet his novel offers in literary form many of the questions occupying theorists of hypertext. There is no denying that digital communication poses a serious challenge to print's dominance over the last couple of centuries. Its arrival manifests cultural and social transformations as fundamental as those that accompanied the introduction of print in the 1450s.[6] For print, as a new medium for communication, education, and entertainment, symbolized historical change, heralding the division between medieval and modern technology, between the courtly world of letters and the market-oriented society of newspapers, pamphlets, journals, and novels. The gradual appearance of print, therefore, elicited both fear and dread because it symbolized great social change. It is important, of course, not to objectify print—or the computer for that matter—as an autonomous force, acting upon society without being acted upon. The Gutenberg invention appeared in a cluster of changes related to other changes in modernity such as urbanization, industrialization, secularization, and nationalism to name a few. It contributed to as much as it manifested these transformations.

Today we are witnessing the decline of print as a mode of cultural reproduction and as an organizing metaphor, a transformation with enormous implications for literature. Walter Benjamin recognized this decades before the eruption of electronic communication. Printing, he observed, had found in the book "a refuge in which to lead an autonomous existence" but now "is pitilessly dragged out onto the street by advertisements and subjected to the brutal heteronomies of economic chaos" (1978: 77). For print endowed literature with certain attributes: the unchanging text, linear reading, the distance between the author and reader, and the ownership of texts by authors. It made literature objectively real, as something to be bought, borrowed, anthologized, criticized, and evaluated on a mass scale (Kernan 1987: 5).[7] It reified words, converting them into commodities, the possessions of writers whose rights were formally recognized by eighteenth-century intellectual property laws (Ong 1982: 131). Texts began to exist as discrete entities, originating in human imagination rather than, as previously thought, in the chain of intertextual relationships.[8]

These characteristics of print are under siege today.[9] The World Wide Web, with its relentlessly advancing bibliographic references and seemingly endless archives, gives credence to the deconstructive claim that everything is text and to the postmodern representation of reality as simulacrum. With the effective disappearance of boundaries between texts and the closure they implied, one text reaches out to another, creating an unfathomable and "unmapable" wetland of writing.

What does this mean for literature? The computer seems to abandon conceptual systems founded on ideas of center and margin, hierarchy and linearity, and to replace them with those based on multilinearity, nodes, links, and networks (Landow 1992: 2). It is giving way to a new mode of textuality, the hypertext. Originally coined by Theodor H. Nelson in the 1960s, hypertext refers to *"nonsequential writing*—text that branches and allows choices to the reader, best read at an interactive screen. As popularly conceived, this is a series of text chunks connected by links which offer the reader different pathways" (Nelson 1992: 0/2). Remarkably prescient, this description captures the protean, referential, and responsive text generated by the computer.[10]

The arrival of the hypertext has been accompanied by an uncritical celebration of its benefits, particularly of its progressive promise for politics and education. Lanham, for instance, claims that electronic publishing is a democratizing process, granting people the capacity to disseminate work not possible before (1993: 10). The enthusiasm for the inexhaustible advantages of cyberspace is best expressed by Mark C. Taylor and Esa Saarinen who hail the "collapse of the literary as a powerbase" and of the "literate project"; they encourage intellectuals to embrace the "images and simulacra" of the hypertext and market their products through the mass media (1994: Section "Philosophy" pp. 15–20).[11] On the whole, the hypertext has transformed the image of the computer in the popular imagination from a means of Orwellian control in the Cold War to today's utopian panacea (Turner 2006: 2).

This digital determinism, however, suggests erroneously that our time is exceptional, giving the impression that we are at the precipitous end of an era. An apocalyptic shadow hangs over these discussions.[12] Yet we are not unique in having espoused such chiliastic thought (Kermode 1966). A look back into history shows us that the introduction of information technologies was accompanied by prophecies of both doom and progress.

The appearance of writing itself provoked excitement and dread, as Plato shows in *Phaedrus*. The god Theuth, who had discovered the art, considered it an "elixir" to make Egyptians wiser. The king, Thamus, however, countered that it would lead to "forgetfulness in the souls of those who have learned it, through lack of practice at using their memory

. . . as through reliance on writing they are reminded from outside by alien marks, not from within, themselves by themselves" (2005: 275a5). During the Reformation people condemned print as a destabilizing force while others saw great advantages in print literacy, regarding it as a step in the amelioration of the human condition. Commentators similarly projected onto radio a utopian vision. Graham Meikle quotes writers from the 1920s and 1930s who celebrated the progressive possibility of radio. They claimed radio would revitalize citizen-based democracy, facilitate crossborder communication, and help people transcend national, racial, and ethnic differences (2002).[13]

The Hype of Hypertext

Cybertheorists predict that hypertext will overtake print because the latter remains in the black-and-white, joyless world of Lutheranism. Linear, fixed, devoid of sound and color, it is a medium of "perceptual self-denial" (Lanham 1993: 73). Print seems difficult, too distanced from ordinary language, but more important, "in its sole appeal to the imagination, [it is] too abstract, too puritanical, too removed from the full range of sensual experience that life affords" (Tuman 1992: 126).

The playful and sensual dimension of on-line literacy makes it the easy winner in the competition for readers. "There is no escaping the fact that there is just lots more to do—more fun to have—with a computer, starting with the simple task afforded by graphics-based operating systems of controlling on the screen the appearance as well as the content of the text" (Tuman 127). Hypertext is "more fun and engaging, than one might suppose before trying it" (Coover 1993: 10). This is so because hypertext incorporates graphic elements, employs font changes to identify various voices and plot twists, and includes hitherto unorthodox elements, such as statistical charts, song lyrics, baseball cards, police reports, board games, and so on.[14]

Robert Coover predicts that in the Net-aesthetic there will be no place for books. Digital information will consign books to those "unattended museums we now call libraries" (1992: 1). The hypertext will finally undo the "author-directed movement from the beginning of a sentence to its period, from the top of the page to the bottom, from the first page to the last" (1). It will unshackle readers from "the tyranny of the line" and the "domination of the author" (23).[15]

This talk of bibliocide, however, is based on the teleological assumption that digital technology is inherently superior to traditional forms of writing and will supplant print much as mammals took over dinosaurs or the car replaced the horse and carriage. Yet, pioneering technologies do not always obliterate previous modes of communication. They can overlap. Television destroyed neither books nor radio, despite predictions. The Darwinian argument is even more precarious when applied to cultural or aesthetic works, which have no utilitarian value and which, therefore, are not susceptible to obsolescence. The modernist experimentation in the early twentieth century did not wipe out inherited narrative in high or popular literature. Traditional lyric written by Edgar Bowers, Thom Gunn, and Dick Davis exists alongside the prevalence of free verse. Not every contemporary author adopts the postmodern techniques of Don DeLillo, Thomas Pynchon, or John Fowles.

It may seem obvious to some critics that students would prefer to surf the Web (or Maui for that matter) rather than working their way through *Middlemarch*. But how will the Internet liberate them? Hypertext is, of course, nonsequential, allowing the reader to explore different pathways within the same text but also in the huge storehouse of information. The computer has already become the great library of libraries, as fantasized about by bibliophiles from Apollonius to Borges. In such a library "'different' articles and books will more likely be *different versions of the same work* and *different pathways through it for different people*" (Nelson 1992: 1/15).

This prophetic characterization of the cyberarchive by Theodor Holm Nelson, however, actually shows how much hypertext theory is indebted to modernist and premodernist reflection on textuality. For the Web library resembles attempts by Mallarmé and Flaubert to imagine the book of books that would contain everything and nothing at the same time. Mallarmé, for instance, aspired to the *Grand Oeuvre*, an "architectural and premeditated" volume that would exist autonomously without being authored by a single individual and would beget itself like language, inexhaustibly producing different versions of itself (1945: 663, 33, 500). Flaubert envisioned an impersonal book devoid of authors, one composed of imperceptible signifiers that were held together by their own density: "a book without an external link, which would sustain itself by the internal force of its style, as the earth retains itself in the air without being supported, a book which would hardly have a subject, or where at least the subject would almost be invisible, if that were possible" (1974: XIII,

158). He endeavored to give actual form to these ideas in his unfinished *Bouvard and Pécuchet* ([1881] 1976) on which he worked until his death in 1880.

Flaubert's novel provides a cautionary tale about the promises of new technologies to revolutionize our lives, showing the vanity of the protagonists' quest for epistemological salvation. Convinced of their ignorance, Bouvard and Pécuchet begin a series of forays into the infinitely receding realm of knowledge. Each chapter starts with their attempt to master a particular discipline and ends in failure which, rather than defeating them, propels them to consult more books to satisfy their hunger for information. As they move from one discourse to another, they discover yet more they need to know. So they resolve to become copyists, resorting ironically to a profession that characterized writing before Gutenberg. Yet, at the same time they are prophetically postmodern, in that, preoccupied with surface, they begin work on the flat, double-sided desk they had specially ordered for this project (288). The Internet promises to make all readers into Bouvards and Pécuchets, beguiling them with informational gratification but also threatening them with informational overload. Each click leads to another window, as an infinite progression into a mirror.

Critics see the multiple circuitry of hypertext as an advance over the single-lane world of print. They also believe that it offers hopes of equality between reader and writer, as was the case of Pavić. In hypertext, both will become "co-learners" or "co-writers," as it were, "fellow travelers in the mapping and remapping of textual (and visual, kinetic and aural) components, not all of which are provided by what used to be called the author" (Coover 1992: 23).

Central to discourse on hypertext is the presumed value of choice. That readers should have maximum freedom in reading patterns is accepted as given, as is the assumption that all readers would prefer such textuality. Michael Joyce, a leading theorist and practitioner of hypertext writing, sees sequential options as the most important characteristic of hypertext fiction. While acknowledging that multidirectionality is basic to hypertext, he adds that "hypertext is reading and writing in an order you *choose* where your *choices* change the nature of what you read . . . Your *choices*, not the author's representations or the initial topography, constitute the current state of the text. You become the reader-as-writer" (1995: 177, my emphasis). The "choice" here has less to do with interpretation—how you understand a word, image, or paragraph—

than with your literal progression through the text—how you negotiate through the windows, highlighted words, or colored nodes. The reader is an Oedipus at the crossroads, solving the Sphinx's riddle before deciding which road to take. Hypertext for Joyce is a "representation of the text that escapes and surprises by turns" (2000: 132), the hallmark, one might add, of all literature. Each page simultaneously dazzles and intimidates readers with a huge web of trails.

Instead of pathways, however, Michael Joyce speaks of stars. Hypertext fiction "spawns galaxies" where constellations link and spin, showering the reader with possibilities. In this electoral rain, readers understandably long to revisit previous groupings, to take stock and catch their breath. To be sure, all reading depends on returning over previous terrain, on rereading. But the protean nature of hypertext frustrates this desire. "In a sufficiently complex and richly contingent hypertext," Joyce explains, "it is impossible to reread even a substantial portion of the possible sequences. [. . .] It is unlikely that successive readings by a single reader will be any significant way alike" (1997: 583). In a sense the reader can never place his finger on the same text twice.

Joyce put his theoretical reflections into practice in "Afternoon: A Story," regarded as the first hypertext fiction, which made its debut in 1987.[16] While Michael Joyce provides readers with some instructions as they install the disk, he remains vague about what happens next. "The lack of clear signals isn't an attempt to vex you, rather an invitation to read either inquisitively or playfully or at depth. Click on words that interest you or invite you." The emphasis is on selection and indeterminacy, as it is in Pavić. For one decision is not necessarily better than the other. The story, Joyce explains in prefatory notes, "exists at several levels and changes according to the decisions you make. A text you have seen previously may be followed by something new, according to a choice you make or already have made during any given reading" (1987).

"Afternoon" achieves electronically what experimental modernist texts and later postmodern fiction strived for in print, the evasion of closure. The collapse of time, the absence of linear narrative, the appearance of flat, two-dimensional protagonists in place of the autonomous, fleshy characters of realist prose, the lack of recognizable setting, the dearth of indexical features guiding the reader, the use of interior monologue, the creation of a poetic, otherworldly atmosphere, the abrupt appearance of characters, the unannounced entry into the mind of a person—all these disorient the reader much as James Joyce's *Ulysses*, Alain Robbe-Grillet's *In the Labyrinth*, and Nikos Pentzikis's *O Pethamenos kai i Anastasi* (The Dead Man and the Resurrection).[17] But "Afternoon" goes beyond modernist fiction, letting the reader travel through the story in a quasi-physical sense, playing with the distinction between a corporeal reality and the illusions of fiction in a different type of parabasis altogether.

Thus by simply hitting "return," the reader may follow the narrative of the protagonist, Peter, who tries to determine whether he has in fact witnessed a traffic accident involving his wife, Lisa, and son, Andrew. Did Peter really see the accident or did he cause it? As the reader steers through the 539 lexias (sections or pages) that make up the story, he has no way of answering this question with any certainty. One link loops to another with further questions and ambiguities. Some links deliberately send the reader back, forcing him to reread. Closure is perennially forestalled. Each reading yields a "different chronology, different apparent motivations, and even a different set of events " (Douglas 1994: 169).[18]

While "Afternoon" is written in the traditional black-and-white mode of print, Michael Joyce's "Twelve Blue. Story in Eight Bars" (n.d.), a languid flow of words and images, incorporates color. In the initial "page" the reader confronts a blue background, within which floats a smaller dark screen containing a series of multicolored threads proceeding horizontally. On a bar below, resembling a ruler, run the numbers one to eight. To the left a vertical bar bears the title and eight two-digit numbers.

Even with the first screen the reader is left with a sense of vertigo, having been thrown into this pool without introduction to character, time, or setting. She reads the text by clicking either on one of the colored threads or any highlighted words. Each thread tells the story of a character but, as the thread slowly disappears by itself, the reader is directed to another narrative. Although it is possible to return to a previous page, the reader cannot retrace the original path because the author has not provided her a spool of twine to follow her way back. More frightening is the reader's discovery that she does not have an ultimate aim—say, to kill the minotaur. The text plays with the reader's expectation of an ending. But does it free readers from the black-and-white cell of print?

Is reading a monastic activity during which we follow the dictates of the author/abbot? In praising the liberating aspect of hypertext and the open work, critics do not sufficiently distinguish between sequential and hermeneutic freedom, however, assuming that readers moving along a linear narrative are trapped in the train of interpretation. This point, which confuses surface reality with hermeneutic freedom, is too obvious to require much discussion. A traditional text, like Euripides' "Medea," which follows the Aristotelian logic of beginning, middle, and end, contains knots of tension that cannot be undone definitively: foe versus friend, barbarian versus Greek, man versus woman, revenge versus compassion, duty versus love. The audience is compelled to choose between different but seemingly irreconcilable accounts. Even though Medea is picked up by a chariot and taken to Athens—in a literal *deus ex machina*—the ideological oppositions that she abandons in Corinth give the play its drama. To claim that the "Medea" is closed because the protagonist is plucked out of the scene while Mark Amerika's Web novel, *Grammatron* (n.d.), is open because of its infinite sequential patterning, is to make a superficial judgment. There remain conflicts in works of art that can never be resolved, which is what makes them art in the first place.

That print is permanent in a physical sense, in contrast to the runny flow of hypertext, should not fool us into believing that it cements the reader into a particular position. The thousands of interpretations of Homer and the Bible over two millennia should dispel the notion that books close off reading. "The dialogue," noted Paul de Man, "between work and interpreter is endless" (1983: 32). It is simplistic to argue that because print compels readers to move from left to right and beginning to end somehow jails them. Such a position represents the (printed) text as a fixed entity, a move reminiscent of the way theorists in the 1970s and 1980s conceived of "closed" works.

They, like hypertext theorists today, lauded the virtues of polyphonic, multidimensional works. Perhaps the most influential was Roland Barthes's masterful *S/Z* (1977), an analysis of Balzac's short story, "Sarrasine." The explication of this text allowed Barthes to make the distinction between readerly (i.e., closed) and writerly (i.e., open) texts. Umberto Eco similarly praised in *The Open Work* "works in movement," "stripped of necessary and foreseeable conclusions" and incorporating "indeterminacy" in their structure (1989: 19).[19]

Whether acknowledged or not, these studies turned out to be a defense of modernist writing, which manifested the qualities of writerly works and which, in fact, anticipated much of the thinking on the topic. These discussions raised important issues about reading, closure, and the hermeneutic act. Left unanswered, however, was the question regarding the practical implications of the distinction between open and closed works of literature. This is significant because underscoring the contrast is an aesthetic and moral evaluation. To be sure, the argument of the end of books, literature, and print, is based in part on the essential boundlessness of the open work and the computer text.

From a historical and descriptive point of view, the differences between nineteenth- and twentieth-century fiction, print narrative and hypertext, are beyond dispute. Does this mean, however, that (from a hermeneutic perspective) one is inherently closed and the other inherently open? One of the great lessons of poststructuralist theory, particularly deconstruction, is that all communication is undecidable, not just that conducted through literary experimentation or on the computer screen. "A signifier is from the very beginning the possibility of its own repetition, of its own image or semblance" (Derrida 1974: 91). This metaphoricity of language suggests that real closure is impossible at the most basic, linguistic level. A degree of unreadability then exists in all works of literature, which has to do less with the richness of meaning than with the properties of language (Hillis Miller 1980: 113). Closure could not be realized aesthetically even if nineteenth-century realist theory claimed to have achieved it. By demonstrating that "Sarrasine" constituted a linguistic and aesthetic construct rather than a slice of life, Barthes showed that realist fiction is itself a fiction. James Wood is right in saying that all great realists are also great formalists (1974: 247).

Moreover, all reading remains an active process. Readers pick up texts with certain expectations about genre and storytelling.[20] They also identify and judge characters according to their own belief structures, engaging with the work in an intricate manner, bringing to bear upon it a variety of intentions, expectations, and aims. Reading, whether of realist or experimental work, requires much intellectual, emotional, and aesthetic investment. All reading involves meaning making, and all reading is an interactive process.

Hypertext implicates the reader more consciously in writing only insofar as it offers a choice in sequences. More to the point, hypertext writing does not liberate readers from all conventions of reading but only from *some* associated with print. As any social construction, it entangles readers in its own web of protocols. Beholden to modernist conceptualizations of textuality, hypertext continues modernist experimentation with its interactive use of print, motion, and color. As such, it brings attention to itself and to print as medium. We begin to be aware of text not only as a semiotic system but also as a physical artifact (Hayles 2002: 29). While it claims to shatter *The Golden Bowl*, turning the pieces into tiny bits of electronic information devoid of body, it is essentially another literary genre. Hypertext makes sense as a critique of the printed text rather than as its successor.

Transitions

It is, of course, perilous to forecast the future. The book may indeed disappear as a treasury of knowledge to be replaced by the Web with its promises of limitless space and dizzyingly fast retrieval. It may also withdraw to the margins as the dominant metaphor by which we warehouse information. The book, Jerome McGann explains, has served two purposes, to store data and to construct simulations, with the first function being informational and the second aesthetic (2001: 168). Digital technology may indeed take over both occupations in the future. This does not mean that the aesthetic or literature will disappear. The hard task remains in figuring out how they will manifest themselves in the digital age.

Janet H. Murray writes that "there are probably not two more difficult things to predict in this world than the future of art and the future of software" (1997: 284). It is challenging to imagine the type of art that can emerge from the computer. Few people could have foretold after the invention of the printing press, for instance, the eventual appearance of the great European novels of the nineteenth century. We face a comparable situation today. Undeniably artists will use the digital technology to develop works that explore the problems and modes of existence of their age, as hypertext authors have already started to do.

When more such works appear, we will no doubt see them as art in another medium. If history is a guide, we will still have to defend them to students, the city school boards, and the public at large. A key point in this defense will be that art electrifies the dividing line between reality and the imagination. This will become more important if, in the worst dreams or nightmares of science fiction, we arrive at a world where the distinction between corporeal reality and computer simulation blurs completely. If we are indeed entering the domain of the posthuman as enacted in the film, *The Matrix*, where consciousness becomes just another computer program, art must continue to bring attention to the boundary between verity and fantasy.

Hypertext literature, of course, addresses this very filament between truth and untruth, pushing this line even further by allowing readers to amble through the illusions of literature in a semiphysical sense. In so doing, this type of fiction only reinforces the art's parabatic potential. With its interdisciplinary promise, hypertext narrative is perfectly suited to exploit the parabatic potential of literature by transforming the old tension between verity and invention into a conflict between the real and the virtually real. The computer can, in other words, develop the parabatic in unforeseen directions, both formal and thematic.

What we are witnessing today, therefore, is less the death of literature than a shift from one technology to another, a transition from one art form to a new one. Aristophanes' *The Frogs* (1962) stages such a shift as a contest between two types of tragedy, each representing diverging conceptions of society and culture. In portraying the movement from one aesthetic to another, Aristophanes also points to the evolution from Old to New Comedy, from political satire to a comedy of manners. In short, we have seen today's combat between narrative and database before but in other forms: in Aristophanes as an agon between two modes of the tragic and in Plato as the struggle between orality and literacy.

Many literary works have addressed these transformations. Hölderlin's "destitute time" is exactly this age of changeover, bidding farewell to the poet as seer while nervously awaiting the professionalized artist. Balzac's *Lost Illusions* (1997) reflects on the consequences of this development. His protagonists mourn the commoditization of poetry in nineteenth-century France. Like Gissing's *New Grub Street* (1891), it shows art in flux, forced to adapt to changing conditions around it and itself contributing to this transformation.

James Joyce's entire oeuvre manifests this revolution from the traditional aesthetics of *A Portrait of the Artist as Young Man* to the radicalism of *Ulysses*. The early novel ends with Stephen Daedalus making a diary entry in which he announces his departure from Dublin to encounter "the reality of experience and to forge in the smithy of my soul the uncreated conscience of my race" (1976: 253). This line points to the odyssey of *Ulysses* made possible by the literary experimentation of modernism. "Are you condemned to do this?" the narrator asks in the ninth chapter of *Ulysses*. Here Stephen is faced with a dialectic, between a single-eyed rendition of the world, as displayed in *Portrait*, and the untried kaleidoscope of *Ulysses*.

A novel form is announced here, recalling W. B. Yeats's poem, "A Coat," in which he casts away the rich vestments of Irish mythology in favor of the here and now. "I made my song a coat / Covered with embroideries / Out of old Mythologies." But after seeing that this attempt to reach a pre-Catholic past actually ignored the political strife of today, he lets the "fools" have his coat. "For there's more enterprise / In walking naked" (1962: 50).

Works of literature have often anticipated the evolution from one mode of writing to another. Ezra Pound's "Hugh Selwyn Mauberley" (1920) dramatizes the switch from symbolism and aestheticism to modernism. Moving from the first to the second sections of the poem, we observe Pound's own self-fashioning as well as the migration from a familiar poetics to the avant-garde. As Pound bids farewell to Edwardian London, "the obstinate isles," he jettisons his inherited notion of poetry (2003: 549).

The poem, however, portrays this journey in both content and form. The first part, written in the poetic discourse of the late nineteenth century, seems like a eulogy to this dying art. "For three years, out of key with his time, / He strove to resuscitate the dead art / Of poetry." On the one hand, the poet senses that the age required a "prose kinema," a new rupture of energy. But, on the other, he recognizes that the age decrees "to kalon" (beauty) in the market place (550). "The stylist has taken shelter, / Unpaid, uncelebrated" (555). But the poet seeks and is capable of radical style, poetry in motion, so he sets off in search of his Persephone (558). Remarkably in the course of the second section he arrives at this new aesthetic. Pound rewrites the poem with a more economic, tighter, and cinematic poetics, exchanging the funereal decadence of the late nineteenth century for the "phantasmagoria," "half-watt rays," "metal," and "topaz" of the twentieth century (563). We enter a fresh medium. "Make it new," Pound proclaims.

How do you make it new? Richard Wagner stages this transformation in *Die Meistersinger von Nürnberg*, his only comic opera and the longest one ever written. The work, first performed in Munich in 1868, deals with the appearance of an original musical idiom as a struggle against the rules and prohibitions of established convention.[21] Like Aristophanes' *Frogs*, it stages an agon between two schools, the rigid orthodoxy of the mastersinger, Sixtus Beckmesser, and the Dionysian energy of the knight, Walther von Stolzing. The contest is not just about who is the better singer and who will win the hand of the beautiful Eva. It concerns the essential place of art in society. For Eva's father, the mastersinger, Veit Pogner, decides to sponsor the poetic contest for her hand to demonstrate the significance of art in Germany. He wants to show that burghers like him around the country "love art in every form" (1980: 366). In a sense Wagner's work performs the perennial tension between "naïve" and "sentimental" art. Wagner is the self-conscious artist par excellence reflecting on a traditional poetic tradition, the stuff of the street and festival, the songs of lovers and worshipers.

This opposition is manifested in the contest between Beckmesser and Walther. When in Act One Walther performs the song he hopes will gain for him admission into the guild of the Nürenberger Mastersingers, Beckmesser serves as the Marker, who records Walther's every mistake, striking each violation of the rules piercingly with his chalk. Hans Sachs, recognizing the beauty and newness of Walther's song, rises to persuade the other masters of Walther's genius. But the masters, frozen in disciplinary narrow-mindedness, refuse to accept Walther as their own. It is only at the end that Walther, singing at the Festival of St. John, moves the hearts of the people, who are not beholden to the masters' conventions, thereby winning both the contest and Eva's hand.

Wagner, the modern artist, composes an opera about art before art's functional differentiation. But is this the end of art, when opera achieves Hegelian self-awareness? Undoubtedly the Wagnerian work is not the "spontaneous" song of the boulevard and meadows. But Wagner shows that there is no purity before autonomy, as even the songs of the guilds were subject to the most codified rules and prohibitions.

Walther introduces an innovative poetic idiom that itself may one day die. What remains, however, is the song. Or, as Cavafy reminds us in "Darius," the wave between imagining and being never dies. In his dry, prosaic language, so unlike Walther's lyricism, Cavafy reflects on the poetic task. Relying on indirect discourse, the speaker attempts to get into the mind of the fictitious poet, Phernazis, who in turn is trying to figure the thoughts of Darius. When Phernazis learns that the Romans have crossed into Cappadocia, he despairs at the overthrow of King Mithridates, for whom he is composing his poem about Darius. How will the king be bothered with poetry in a time of political turmoil? "Imagine Greek poetry in the midst of a war!" But Phernazis just cannot give up on art. "The poetic idea comes and goes insistently" (Cavafy 1963 II: 18–19). We may perhaps surmise the reasons for his aesthetic optimism by looking at his goal. Phernazis was attempting in his epic to represent Darius's thinking, the ancestor of king Mithridates, as he had ascended to the Persian throne:

He has to figure out
the feelings Darius would have had:
Maybe arrogance and intoxication. Not really. Maybe
a sense of the vanity of greatness. (18)

Perhaps Phernazis has come to comprehend that the Roman rulers would at the end require his talents. They may discover the benefit of putting themselves into the mind of another person, the necessity of capturing the emperor's "passions," his "frown, and wrinkled lip, and sneer of cold command," as Shelley put it, writing about the hubristic Ozymandias. Possibly this is what Hans Sachs has in mind when he tells Walther "all book-craft and all poetry / Are naught but dreams made verity" (Wagner 1980: 407). When a few lines later he says that Walther's verses are so supreme, he cannot tell "how much was poetry, how much dream," Sachs finds the magic of parabasis. We will always look for that fluid thread between life and illusion, that line, the lie that is the poem.

Notes

Preface

1. For example, Elaine Scarry (1999), Wendy Steiner (2001), Stathis Gourgouris (2003), Jonathan Loesberg (2005), Charles Martindale (2005), Alexander Nehamas (2007), Myra Jehlen (2008), Jay Parini (2008), James Wood (2008), and the anthologies by George Levine (1994), James Soderholm (1997), Pamela R. Matthews and David McWhitler (2003), and John J. Joughin and Simon Malpas (2003).

Chapter 1

1. Niklas Luhmann characterizes functional specialization as one of the few constant elements in the history of sociology (2000: 133). It signifies the occupational segmentation of society by which various human activities became grouped into separate categories (religion, education, the state, the economy, and the bureaucracy) as analyzed by Marx, Weber, and Durkheim.

2. The modern Greek *logotechnia* appeared in the early nineteenth century to signify the general category of literature, replacing the narrow *poiisis* (poetry). See my *Belated Modernity and Aesthetic Culture* (1991).

3. Obviously the boundaries are fluid. Literary texts often play with this tension between the literary and nonliterary. But we should note that, although a poem may present itself as a laundry list, few people would take a poem to the cleaners.

4. Lukács's motivation for writing *The Theory of the Novel* was the outbreak of World War I. He saw the problem of the novel as mirroring the problem of the "world gone out of joint" (1971: 17).

5. Yet 9/11 novels have appeared: Jonathan Safran Foer's *Extremely Loud and Incredibly Close* (2005), Ian McEwan's *Saturday* (2005), and Claire Messud's *The Emperor's Children* (2006).

6. See Edmund Burke's *Philosophical Inquiry into the Origin of Our Ideas of the Sublime and Beautiful* ([1756] 1873).

7. One is reminded here of the opening to Rilke's first Duino Elegy: "Beauty's nothing / but the start of terror we can hardly bear, / and we adore it because of the serene score / it could kill us with" (1955: 5).

8. Wendy Steiner has shown how modernist artists employed the sublime as a weapon to devalue beauty (2001). We demote beauty, Elaine Scarry notes, when we turn our eyes away from the "meadow flowers" to the "august silence of ancient groves" (1999: 84).

9. See "Are Book Reviewers out of Print?" *New York Times* May 2, 2007, (B1).

10. More than fifteen years earlier Nicholas Zill and Marianne Winglee came to similar conclusions in their analysis of American publishing (1989).

11. See Alonso (2003), Crewe (2004), Lewis (2002, 2004), MLA (2002) and Murrell (2001).

12. In his tenure as the director of the Literature Program of the National Endowment for the Arts under George W. H. Bush, Joe David Bellamy heard three arguments in defense of federal support for the arts: economic, social, and pedagogic. They stimulate tourism and promote civic pride; they can ameliorate the effects of poverty and racial inequality; they lead to better performance in academic subjects (1992: 669).

13. The essays appeared in *PMLA* 117: 3 (2002): 487–522. A similar anthology appeared six years later on the significance and place of lyric in the undergraduate curriculum. *PMLA* 123: 1 (2008): 181–234.

14. See "Fiction Losing Status in Schools" *Columbus Dispatch* April 23, 2007, (A1). The article's subtitle is telling: "Nonfiction Better Preparation for Tests, Life."

15. See also Mark Edmundson (1995).

16. The list of complaints is long. Winfried Fluck refers to the frequent dismissal of aesthetic concerns in literary studies (2002: 79–80). Those who speak about the literariness of texts, Heinz Ickstadt argues, often appear reactionary (2002: 263). Marc William Roche worries that we neglect normative questions such as "What is Art?" "Why should we read and teach literature?" (2004: 10).

17. See also Danto (1997). J. Hillis Miller saw similar lessons in the fading of literature as a cultural force in the late twentieth century. "The efflorescence of literary theory signals the death of literature" (2002: 35).

18. One can point to the Parthenon marbles in the British Museum as an illustration of Hegel's point. They embellish the museum rather than glorifying a temple. On the Greek perception of sculpture, see Shiner (2001: 25–26).

19. Compare Spengler's dire association of modern society with the decline of Rome (1926–28: 40) to Fukuyama's ebullient prediction that "at the end of

history there are no serious ideological competitors left to liberal democracy" (1992: 211). See Cooper (1984), Niethammer (1992), and Christensen (2000).

20. Kant believed that after the many wars and "reformative revolutions" this cosmopolitan civic society would be achieved in which "all the original capacities of the human race can develop" (2001: 23).

21. From a different point of view, David Simpson explores how storytelling has migrated from this genre to other disciplines and popular culture, yielding the confessional and conversational modes of postmodernism (1995).

22. The play, part of Stoppard's trilogy, "The Coast of Utopia," explores the romantics and revolutionaries in nineteenth-century Russia.

Chapter 2

1. Culture in general is in the same situation, often regarded as a derivative force in society, reacting to changes rather than generating them itself, overshadowed by more influential forces such as the economy or the state. I have dealt with this at greater length in *The Necessary Nation* (2001). See also Butler 1998.

2. Plato had as his target the centrality of literary study in Athens and the overwhelming importance of drama and poetry in social life (Levin 2001: 9). In order to show the dominance of philosophy he had to undermine poetry's privileged position. In so doing, he saw the two as separate modes of discourse.

3. Poets, Horace wrote in "Ars Poetica," should "benefit" and "amuse," being "at once both pleasing and helpful to life" (1929: 479).

4. Clement Greenberg made similar arguments for modern art, decrying confusion of genres and calling for sharper distinctions among arts, with each art focused on its own resources and medium (1985).

5. See Timothy J. Reiss (2002). For the opposite perspective see Lansdown (2001).

6. A notable example is Louis Kampf, the president of the Modern Language Association in 1971, who spoke of literature as an "instrument of social elitism," a tool of "class differentiation," and a "weapon in the hands of imperialism" (1970: 28, 31); see also Kampf (1969).

7. See Lambropoulos (1988). Those who reject Arnold as a defender of social privilege often forget that he was reacting to the commercialization of art. The cultivation of the mind, he insisted, "is at variance with the mechanical and material civilization in esteem with us, and no where . . . so much in esteem as with us" (38). Ryle and Soper see Arnold's *Culture and Anarchy* as a reflection on the place of "learned culture," historically the preserve of elites, in a time of commodification (2002: 4).

8. As others have amply described this rejection of the aesthetic (see Chapter One), I need not spend time on it here.

9. Sarah Kay shows how literature was indeed treated this way in the twelfth century (2001).

10. On the role of the press in the period leading to the war, see Frank Rich's *The Greatest Story Ever Sold* (2006).

11. On the antiaesthetic of postmodernism, see Foster (1983) and Grabes (1995).

12. Koons created a 10-foot, stainless steel sculpture of a twisted balloon dog. The Broad Art Foundation, Santa Monica.

13. See here Duve's *Pictorial Nominalism* (1991).

14. Literature became a consumable good in Germany at least around the 1840s when the book market was commodified (Hohendahl 1989). On the commodification of English fiction see Lovell (1987), on the visual arts see Wartofsky (1980), and on music see Attali (1985).

15. Important here is also Neil Postman's work (1985).

16. Winckelmann may have idealized Athenian society but was not off the mark when he argued that it prized beauty greatly. It was the self-governance of Athens, he wrote, that created the superiority of its art ([1764] 1968 1/2: 179).

17. In his penultimate diary entry, Stephen speaks of encountering "the reality of experience" (Joyce 1976: 253). It is remarkable how traditional Stephen's aesthetic theories are in *A Portrait of the Artist as a Young Man* when compared with the radicalism of *Ulysses*, published six years later. *Portrait* marks the transition from inherited poetics to experimental modernism.

Chapter 3

1. "Life is earnest. Art is light-hearted" (Schiller 1901: 45).

2. See Mendelsohn (1929 [1757]) and Moritz (1962 [1785]). See also Wood-mansee (1984).

3. Before the eighteenth century, aesthetic theories did not always distinguish between manuals to poets in writing poetry and to readers in judging it (Abrams 1985: 18–19).

4. The concept of disinterestedness was conceived by Lord Shaftsbury (1671–1713) in the context of his ethics and then applied to a theory of beauty. Other British thinkers, such as Joseph Addison (1672–1719) and Francis Hutcheson (1694–1746), took it up. So did Moritz. Kant used it to give his argument universality, namely that the aesthetic judgment was triggered by a common human feature, rather than by individual wants. See Abrams (1981) and Stolnitz (1961a, 1961b).

5. David Hume (1711–76) wrote that "beauty is no quality in things themselves: it exists merely in the mind which contemplates them; and each mind

perceives a different beauty" ([1741–42] 1963: 234). Hume strove for a "standard of taste" by which various sentiments could be reconciled. Henry Home (1696–1782) argued against the existence of one "standard of taste," as it changed from one person to another. ([1761] 1867: 482). Kant wanted to avoid this apparent relativism.

6. On this see also Zammito (1992).

7. I am referring here to Bourdieu's critique of Kant (1984). How to interpret Kant's aesthetics—whether as a progressive contribution to our understanding of art or as a regression to be overcome—has divided thinkers for a century (McCormick 1990). George Dickie dismisses Kant as an obtuse thinker (1996).

8. On the relationship between these cultural phenomena and general political processes, see Timothy Blanning's study (2002).

9. On the nationalization of literature see Hohendahl (1989) for Germany, Jusdanis (1991) for Greece, Baldick (1983) and Hunter (1988) for England, and Graff (1987) for the United States.

10. Aestheticism also connotes the literary movement at the end of the nineteenth century.

11. In his *History of Ancient Art* ([1764] 1968), Winckelmann tied the superiority of Greek art to the political independence of Athens (179). See Ferris (2000).

12. Rationalization, Max Weber explained, "means that principally there are no mysterious incalculable forces that come into play, but rather that one can, in principle, master all things by calculation. This means that the world is disenchanted" (1946: 139).

13. Ian Hunter analyzes the use of literature in education (1988).

14. On the emergence of the literary agent at this time see Gillies (2007).

15. Those prophesying the death of the book by pointing to hypertext writing may say that Marian's wish is becoming a reality. I return to this in the final chapter.

16. This is discussed by Fontius (1977) and Schulte-Sasse (1989).

17. So did painters. "The ultimate end of painting," insisted the cubist painters Albert Gleizes (1881–1953) and Jean Metzinger (1883–1956), "is to reach the masses" ([1912] 1964: 18). It was their hope that the public would come to understand cubism, despite its opacity.

18. This is the same Wilde who argued that "there may have been fogs for centuries in London . . . But no one saw them, and so we do not do anything about them. They did not exist till art invented them" ([1891] 1945: 30).

19. All translations from Cavafy are my own.

20. Art for art's sake symbolized less the autonomy of art than a weapon against the social and didactic demands of the bourgeoisie (Wellek 1970: 136).

21. I am not engaging here with two major arguments against modernism: its elitism and its marginalization of beauty. See Hickey (1997) and Steiner (2001.)

22. While Bourdieu offers a sharp analysis of the "literary field," he does not acknowledge the work on the institutionality of art by Becker (1982), Christa Bürger (1977), Christa Bürger et al. (1980, 1982), Peter Bürger (1984), Dubois (1978), and Fish (1980).

23. There are antecedents for this conflict. Scholars, like Galileo, struggled to win intellectual freedom from the Catholic Church in the seventeenth century.

24. Although the idea of the artist as social outcast goes back to Romanticism, the conception of the subject as a self-regulating being can be traced to the seventeenth century (Lambropoulos 1993).

25. Luc Ferry sees the history of aesthetics as a "subjectivization of the world" and a progressive inwardness (1993: 19).

26. For a different perspective on this topic, see Crow (1985) and Foss (1971).

27. Critics focused on these later authors when they labeled all of Romanticism reactionary (Blechman 1999: 6). Carl Schmitt, following the lead of Madame de Staël, argued that Romanticism escaped the world through the aestheticization of politics. It romanticized history by turning social life into a pretext for a novel (1986: 83–84). Schmitt's thesis turns out to be yet another attack on art.

28. In the second part of Hölderlin's *Hyperion* the hero partakes in the Greek effort. He rejoices when he learns from his friend Alabanda that "Russia has declared war on the Porte; their fleet is arriving in the Archipelago [in 1770]; the Greeks will be free if they rebel and drive the Sultan to the Euphrates" (1946–1985, III: 94).

29. On Romanticism and revolution, see Blechman (1999), Jusdanis (2002), and Sharpe and Zwicker (1998). One can point to other artists such as Stendahl, who supported national liberation, and Pushkin, who sympathized with political radicals.

Chapter 4

1. I disagree, therefore, with Niklas Luhmann's view of autonomy as absolute. His systems theory suggests that borders are impassable: "Autonomy implies that, within its boundaries, autopoiesis functions unconditionally . . . Autonomy allows for no half-measures or graduation; there are no relative states, no more or less autonomous systems" (2000: 157).

2. Douglas Robinson (2008) examines Shklovsky's notion of defamiliarization in this wider philosophical and literary context. See also Boris Eichenbaum's "The Theory of the Formal Method" (1965).

3. Georgos Ioannou's "The Teacher" (1993) deals with the encounter between a middle-aged woman and her former student. Through long, intricate,

sentences often running an entire paragraph, Ioannou entangles readers in the complexity of a relationship as inconclusive as that described by Welty.

4. Drama, lyric, and the epic are in their own way, Lukács writes, "a means, qualitatively quite heterogeneous from the others, of giving form to the world. Each form appears positive because it fulfills its own structural laws" (1971: 128).

5. This does not make play into a free-flowing pursuit. Huizinga has defined play as an activity conducted "according to rules freely accepted, and outside the sphere of necessity or material utility" (1980: 132). See also Caillois (1961).

6. Zeuxis and Parrhasius, two of the greatest Athenian painters, were involved in a contest to execute the most realistic illusion. After displaying his painting of grapes, Zeuxis was delighted to see birds alighting on his canvas. He then asked Parrhasius to pull the curtain hiding his picture only to realize that this screen was indeed his rival's work. Zeuxis too was deceived but, unlike his feathered victims, he knew this was an artistic agon. Art marks the difference between people and birds.

7. There is something more to this than aesthetics. The neuroscientist, Michael S. Gazzaniga, argues that humans have a specialized system allowing them to enter imaginary worlds. This cognitive structure emerges in children at eighteen months of age and can be impaired by autism. He sees the neural machinery enabling us to enjoy make-believe as an adaptive mechanism. Humans developed the capacity to differentiate fact from fiction as an evolutionary advantage over other creatures, aiding them in their ability to flee predators, determine their relationships to kin and nonkin, or find a mate (2008: 219).

8. They attain an intimacy that we see in Tolstoy's magisterial story, "Master and Man." The egotistical Vasíli, having abandoned his servant, Nikíta, to die in the snowstorm, returns in remorse, falling on top of him like a blanket. "'Nikíta is alive, so I too am alive!' he said to himself triumphantly" (1978: 649). In the morning travelers find Vasíli dead but still covering his servant, who survives.

9. Paul Klee manifests this Aristotelian conception of art when he writes: "I do not wish to represent the man as he is, but only as he might be" ([1924] 1964: 90).

10. See the discussion on p. 40 of Chapter Two.

11. Novelists, Lodge continues, have always explored how to give an "objective" third-person account of a "subjective" first-person experience. Lodge has devoted a novel to this topic, *Thinks: A Novel* (2001). See Wood (2008). On literature's "alternate versions of reality," see Paulson (2001: 121).

12. As such, it explores the parabatic border between fiction and autobiography.

13. Old Comedy, so named by Hellenistic critics, indicates the comic theater of the fifth century of which Aristophanes is the most renowned practitioner.

14. In each dramatic festival, produced at taxpayers' expense, judges chose the best play. Aristophanes was awarded third prize for "Clouds" in 423 BCE.

15. The chorus in the "Frogs" is made up of two groups: (a) frogs who are heard with the famous refrain "brekekekex koax koax" but not seen, and (b) of initiates.

16. It is astonishing that Aristophanes, so eager to win the first prize, considered this metatheoretical discussion a fitting theme for this play. That a debate about the nature of tragedy should be seen as a theme for popular entertainment underscores the high value Athenians placed on tragedy.

17. These hilarious references to quantifying art's worth voice the disquiet of the audience at the controversial rhetorical techniques introduced by sophists to studying poetry, already the object of satire in the "Clouds."

Chapter 5

1. "Not trickery. The stage unveils for us the secret of reality." (Strauss 1942: Act 1)

2. Could we imagine a similar portrayal of the Japanese eight years after the attack on Pearl Harbor or a play today about the Taliban's suffering produced in the Kennedy Center at taxpayers' expense?

3. Just before the finale, the Herald suspends the action. Then a musical interlude provides a historical account of the years between 1793 and 1808 (Weiss 1965: 95–96).

4. Although Brecht was working on his "Coriolan," he was, in fact, rehearsing Strittmatter's "Katzgraben" during the strike. But Grass was interested in the ironies of history and the contradictory pulls of stage and life. Coriolanus was the Roman patrician and senator who argued against the democratic aspirations of the plebeians. Brecht, as one of the characters says, hopes "to upgrade the plebeians," making them class conscious (Grass 1966: 6).

5. In a published text, Brecht distanced himself from the state's actions, but ended up expressing his "solidarity with the Socialist Unity Party of Germany" (Grass 1966: 122).

6. In Tom Stoppard's "The Real Thing" (1982), for instance, it is hard to know if individuals are acting their roles or experiencing them as real people. In the opening scene Max discovers the infidelity of his wife, Charlotte. But in the next one, Charlotte is in a bedroom with a man named Henry as Max appears at the door. Gradually we discover that Charlotte is an actress, along with Max, appearing in a play directed by her husband, Henry.

7. What Edmund Wilson said of Joyce holds for Mallarmé: "Joyce's world is always changing as it is perceived by different observers and by them at different times" (1931: 222).

8. In another poem Pessoa captures the inbetweenness of writing: "Best is to neither dream nor not dream and / Unawake without end" (1982: 53).

9. In switching between first and second narration, Zei's novel resembles Nadine Gordimer's *Burger's Daughter*, a work set in apartheid South Africa. The central character is a young woman, Rosemarie Burger, whose parents are involved in the antiapartheid movement. With her mother dead and her father in prison, the novel traces Rosemarie's personal and political experience. This tension between the outside and inside is depicted with the double narration. "My version and theirs," the narrator says. "And if this were written down, both would seem equally concocted when read over. And if I were really telling, instead of talking to you in my mind the way I find I do" (1979: 16).

10. Written with postmodern panache, *Snow* presents the conflicts that fascinate a Western audience about the Middle East, namely the struggle between political Islam and westernizing forces. Like Kazantzakis a half a century earlier, Pamuk portrays a modernizing society with a language and style that Western readers can understand and appreciate. On how international tastes shape and create international authors see my "World Literature: The Unbearable Lightness of Thinking Globally" (Jusdanis 2003).

Chapter 6

1. There is an irony, however, when Ed Folsom describes the relationship between narrative and database as a *battle* (2007: 1575). Doesn't this metaphorical characterization confirm the continued presence of narrative? The makers of computer games, of course, know this. See Vesna (2007). N. Catherine Hayles (2007) counters some of Manovich's arguments.

2. David Damrosch castigates critics for endorsing the book's postmodernist virtuosity while ignoring Pavić's role in the dissolution of Yugoslavia. He analyzes this "poisoned book" as a "cautionary tale" of what happens to world literature when readers disregard the social context of the novel (2003). Damrosch bases his reading on an article by Andrew Wachtel who, with little sensitivity to postmodern irony, investigates Pavić's role in the "literary demolition of Yugoslavia" (1997: 635, 638). For a more nuanced reading of Pavić's nationalism see Ramadanović (1994) and Mihajlović (1998).

3. On the death of the book see Kurzweil (1999), Joyce (1995), and Odin (1997).

4. Wells's dystopia expresses fin-de-siècle ennui that we have seen in Verlaine and Cavafy. The exquisite buildings the time traveler beholds represent the last surge of human creativity. "This has been the fate of energy in security; it takes to art and to eroticism, and then come languor and decay" (1996: 33).

5. "This drama is not fictional," the narrator says; "it is not a novel. All is true" (Balzac 1994: 5).

6. See Eisenstein (1979), McLuhan (1962), and Siskin (1998).

7. See also Kernan (1990).

8. On originality and the author see Abrams (1953), Bate (1971), and Bloom (1973).

9. On the computer and writing see Bolter (2001), McGann (2001), and Lanham (1993).

10. The hypertext should be distinguished from "ebooks," which are digital versions of either already printed novels or newly created ones. See Glazer (2004).

11. Mark Dery provides a cheerful exploration of cyberspace and cyborgs (1996). For a more sober analysis see Rheingold (2000).

12. See McKibben (1989).

13. When photography appeared in the nineteenth century, some foresaw the end of painting. Rather than expiring, however, painting offered, through Impressionism, insights into experience the camera could not achieve (Schwarz 1985: 90–91).

14. Is this entirely new? Dada poets included nonprint forms in their work, often striking a synthesis of the pictorial, oral, and textual. The chaotic performances at Zurich's Cabaret Voltaire incorporated acting, dancing, and writing.

15. N. Katherine Hayles sees the disappearance of the book in the context of the posthuman and the cyborg. Books are in danger of losing their bodies just like humans (1998, 2002). See also Haraway (1991) and Gray (2001). On hypertext see also Aarseth (1997).

16. Ten years later this and other first-generation hypertexts can't be read as they are no longer compatible with new computer systems (Fitzpatrick 2008: 720). Is it ironic that hypertext has beaten print into obsolescence?

17. Of these three novels, Robbe-Grillet's is the closest in mood, atmosphere, and characterization to Michael Joyce's text. *In the Labyrinth* ([1959] 1960) unnamed characters, whose motives are not defined, seem to roam the horizontal, one-dimensional territory. Both texts resist an allegorical interpretation.

18. The possibilities for this type of narrative are limitless in our age of video games. Consider the story of Trip and Grace on <interactivestory.net> where readers, welcomed into the couple's house, type various questions to engage the couple in an argument or conversation. The story changes, depending on the questions fed to the screen.

19. See also Kermode (1966), Friedman (1966), Hillis Miller (1978), Hernnstein-Smith (1968), Turgovnick (1981), and Lambropoulos (1988). On closure see White (1987). Lacoure-Labarthe and Nancy (1988) discuss the fragment as an unfinished work.

20. See Jauss (1982), Iser (1974, 1980), Riffaterre (1973), Todorov (1980), and Fish (1980).

21. In Strauss's *Capriccio* the characters are also in search of an innovative opera. The musician, Flamand, and the poet Olivier, mock the plans of the director, La Roche, to stage traditional theater such as the birth of Athena or the sack of Carthage. "Passé, passé," they shout, calling instead for demotic, lively work (1942: 177).

References

Aarseth, Espen J. 1997. *Cybertext: Perspectives on Ergodic Literature* Baltimore: The Johns Hopkins University Press.

Abrams, M. H. 1953. *The Mirror and the Lamp: Romantic Theory and the Critical Tradition*. Oxford, U.K.: Oxford University Press.

———. 1958. *Literature and Belief.* New York: Columbia University Press.

———. 1981. "Kant and the Theology of Art." *Notre Dame English Journal.* XIII, 3, 75–106.

———. 1985. "From Addison to Kant: Modern Aesthetics and the Exemplary Art" *Studies in Eighteenth-Century British Arts and Aesthetics.* Edited by Ralph Cohen. Berkeley: University of California Press.

Adorno, Theodor W. 1997. *Aesthetic Theory.* Edited and translated by Robert Hullot-Kentor. Minneapolis: University of Minnesota Press.

Aeschylus. 1956. "The Persians." In *Aeschylus II.* Translated by Seth G. Benardete. Chicago: The University of Chicago Press.

Alonso, Carlos J. 2003. "Having a Spine—Facing the Crisis in Scholarly Publishing." *PMLA* 118: 2, 217-223.

Amerika, Mark. Nd. *Grammatron.* www.grammatron.com.

Arendt, Hannah. 1977. *Between Past and Present: Eight Exercises in Political Thought.* New York: Penguin.

Aristophanes. 1958. *The Frogs.* Edited by. W. B. Stanford. London: Macmillan Education.

———. 1962. "The Frogs" in *Four Plays by Aristophanes.* Translated by William Arrowsmith. New York: Penguin.

———. 1964. *The Wasps, The Poet and the Women, The Frogs.* Translated by David Barrett. Harmondsworth, U.K.: Penguin.

———. 1973. *Lysistrata, The Acharnians, The Clouds.* Translated by Alan H. Sommerstein. London: Penguin.

Aristotle. *Poetics*. 1984. Translated by I. Bywater. In *The Complete Works Of Aristotle*, Vol. II. Edited by Jonathan Barnes. Princeton, N.J.: Princeton University Press.

Armstrong, Isobel. 2000. *The Radical Aesthetic*. Oxford, U.K.: Blackwell.

Arnold, Matthew. 1971. *Culture and Anarchy: An Essay in Political and Social Criticism*. Indianapolis: Bobbs-Merrill Co.

Attali, Jacques. 1985. *Noise: The Political Economy of Music*. Translated by Brian Massumi. Minneapolis: University of Minnesota Press.

Attridge, Derek. 2004. *The Singularity of Literature*. New York: Routledge.

Baldick, Chris. 1983. *The Social Mission of English Criticism 1848–1932*. Oxford, U.K.: Oxford University Press.

Balzac, Honoré de. 1994. *Père Goriot*. Translated by Barton Raffel. New York: Norton.

———. 1997. *Lost Illusions*. Translated by Kathleen Raine. New York: Random House.

Barthes, Roland. 1974. *S/Z. An Essay*. Translated by Richard Miller. New York: Hill and Wang.

———. 1977. *Image, Music, Text*. Translated by Stephen Heath. New York: Hill and Wang.

Bate, Walter J. 1971. *The Burden of the Past and the English Poet*. London: Chatto & Windus.

Bateson, Gregory. 1972. *Steps to an Ecology of Mind*. New York: Ballantine Books.

Baudrillard, Jean. 1981. *For a Critique of the Political Economy of the Sign*. Translated by Charles Levin. St. Louis: Telos Press.

———. 1994. *Simulacra and Simulation*. Translated by Sheila Faria Glaser. Ann Arbor: University of Michigan Press.

Baumgarten, Alexander Gottlieb. 1954. *Reflections on Poetry*. Translated by Karl Aschenbrenner and William Holther. Berkeley: University of California Press.

Baxter, Charles. 1997. *Burning Down the House: Essays on Fiction*. Saint Paul, MN: Graywolf Press.

Becker, Howard S. 1982. *Art Worlds*. Berkeley: University of California Press.

Beiser, Frederick C. 1992. *Enlightenment, Revolution, and Romanticism: The Genesis of Modern German Political Thought 1790–1800*. Cambridge, MA: Harvard University Press.

———. 1996. "Introduction." *The Early Political Writings of the German Romantics*. Edited and Translated by Frederick C. Beiser. Cambridge, U.K.: Cambridge University Press.

Bellamy, Joe David. 1992. "On Pens and Swords." *The Nation*. Nov. 30, 668–72.

Belting, Hans. 1987. *The End of the History of Art?* Translated by Christopher S. Wood. Chicago: The University of Chicago Press.

Benjamin, Walter. 1969. *Illuminations*. New York: Schocken Books.

———. 1978. *Reflections*. Translated by Edmund Jephcott. New York: Harcourt Brace Jovanovich.

Bennett, Tony. 1990. *Outside Literature*. London: Routledge.

Bérubé, Michael. 1998. *The Employment of English: Theory, Jobs, and the Future of Literary Studies*. New York: New York University Press.

Blanning, Timothy. 2002. *The Culture of Power and the Power of Culture: Old Regime Europe 1660–1789,* Oxford, U.K.: Oxford University Press.

Blechman, Max. 1999. *Revolutionary Romanticism*. San Francisco: City Lights Books.

Bloom, Harold. 1973. *The Anxiety of Influence: A Theory of Poetry*. New York: Oxford University Press.

———. 1994. *The Western Canon: The Books and School of All Ages*. New York: Harcourt Brace.

Bohls, Elizabeth A. 1995. *Women Travel Writers and the Language of Aesthetics 1716–1818*. Cambridge, U.K.: Cambridge University Press.

Bolter, Jay David. 2001. *Writing Space: Computers, Hypertext, and the Remediation of Print*. 2nd Ed. Mahwah, NJ: Lawrence Erlbaum Associates.

Bourdieu, Pierre. 1984. *Distinction. A social Critique of the Judgment of Taste*. Translated by R. Nice. London: Routledge.

———. 1995. *The Rules of Art: Genesis and Structure of the Literary Field*. Translated by Susan Emanuel. Stanford, CA: Stanford University Press.

Bragg, Melvyn. 2006. *12 Books That Changed the World*. London: Hodder & Stoughton.

Brecht, Bertolt. 1957. *Brecht on Theater. The Development of an Aesthetic*. Translated by John Willett. New York: Hill and Wang.

———. 1976. *Poems 1913–1956*. Edited by John Willett and Ralph Manheim. New York: Methuen.

Bürger, Christa. 1977. *Die Ursprung der bürgerlicher Institutionskunst im Hofischen Weimar*. Frankfurt: Suhrkamp,

Bürger, Christa, Peter Bürger, and Jochen Schulte-Sasse. 1980. *Aufklärung und Literarische Offentlichkeit*. Frankfurt: Suhrkamp,

Bürger, Christa, Peter Bürger, and Jochen Schulte-Sasse. 1982. *Zur Dichotomisierung von hoher und niederer Literatur*. Frankfurt: Suhrkamp.

Bürger, Peter. 1984. *Theory of the Avant-Garde*. Translated by Michael Shaw. Minneapolis: University of Minnesota Press.

———. 1985/86. "The Institution of 'Art' as a Category in the Sociology of Literature." *Cultural Critique* 2, 5–33.

Burke, Edmund. 1873. *Philosophical Inquiry into the Origin of Our Ideas of the Sublime and Beautiful with an Introductory Discourse Concerning Taste.* New York: Harper Brothers.

Butler, Judith. 1998. "Merely Cultural." *New Left Review.* No. 227, Jan./Feb. 33–44.

Byron, George Gordon. 1936. *Childe Harold's Pilgrimage and Other Romantic Poems.* Edited by Samuel C. Chew. New York: The Odyssey Press.

Caillois, Roger. 1961. *Man, Play, and Games.* Translated by Meyer Barash. New York: Free Press.

Carroll, David. 1989. *Paraesthetics: Foucault, Lyotard, Derrida.* New York: Routledge.

Carver, Raymond. 1983. *Cathedral. Stories.* New York. Knopf.

Cascardi, Anthony. 1991. "Aesthetic Liberalism: Kant and the Ethics of Modernity." *Revue Internationale de Philosophie* 1: 196, 10–23.

———. 1997. "Communication and Transformation: Aesthetics and Politics in Kant and Arendt." In *Hannah Arendt and the Meaning of Politics.* Edited by Craig Calhoun and John McGowan. Minneapolis: University of Minnesota Press.

Cavafy, Constantine P. 1963. *Piimata.* 2 Vols. Edited by George Savidis. Athens: Ikaros.

———. 1977. *Anekdota Piimata.* Edited by George Savidis. Athens: Ikaros.

Chaouli, Michel. 2003. "The Perpetual Conflict in Cultural Studies: An Apology." *Profession 2003.* New York: MLA, 55–65.

Cheever, John. 1978. *The Stories of John Cheever.* New York: Ballantine Books.

Chekhov, Anton. 1960. *Selected Stories.* Translated by Ann Dunnigan. New York: New American Library.

Chinitz, David. 1995. "T. S. Eliot and the Cultural Divide." *PMLA* 110: 2, 236–47.

Chinweizu, Onwuchekwa Jemie and Ihechukwu Madubuike. 1983. *Toward the Decolonization of African Literature.* Vol. 1. Washington, DC: Howard University Press.

Christensen, Jerome. 2000. *Romanticism at the End of History.* Baltimore: The Johns Hopkins University Press.

Chytry, Josef. 1989. *The Aesthetic State: A Quest in Modern German Thought.* Berkeley: University of California Press.

Clark, Michael P. 2000. "Introduction." In *The Revenge of the Aesthetic: The Place of Literature in Theory Today.* Edited by Michael P. Clark. Berkeley: University of California Press.

Cohen, Ted. 1988. "The Very Idea of Art." *NCECA Journal* 9: 1, 7–14.

Cooper, Barry. 1984. *The End of History: An Essay on Modern Hegelianism.* Toronto: University of Toronto Press.

Coover, Robert. 1992. "The End of Books." *New York Times Book Review*, June 21, 1, 23–25.

———. 1993. "Hyperfiction: Novels for the Computer." *New York Times Book Review*, August 29, 1, 8–10.

Le Corbusier and Amédée Ozenfant. 1964. "Purism." In *Modern Artists on Art*. Edited by Robert L. Herbert. Englewood Cliffs, NJ: Prentice-Hall.

Crewe, Jennifer. 2004. "Scholarly Publishing: Why Our Business Is Your Business Too." *Profession 2004*. New York: MLA, 25–31.

Crow, Thomas. E. 1985. *Painters and Public Life in Eighteenth-Century Paris 1660–1750*. New Haven: Yale University Press.

Damrosch, David. 2003. *What Is World Literature?* Princeton: Princeton University Press.

Danto, Arthur C. 1986. *The Philosophical Disenfranchisement of Art*. New York: Columbia University Press.

———. 1997. *After the End of Art: Contemporary Art and the Pale of History*. Princeton, NJ: Princeton University Press.

De Man, Paul. 1983. *Blindness and Insight: Essays in the Rhetoric of Contemporary Criticism*. 2nd ed. Minneapolis: University of Minnesota Press.

———. 1984. "Phenomenality and Materiality in Kant." *Hermeneutics: Questions and Prospects*. Edited by Gary Shapiro and Alan Sica. Amherst: University of Massachusetts Press.

———. 1986. *The Resistance to Theory*. Minneapolis: University of Minnesota Press.

Derrida, Jacques. 1974. *Of Grammatology*. Translated by Gayatri Chakravorty Spivak. Baltimore: The Johns Hopkins University Press.

Dery, Mark. 1996. *Escape Velocity: Cyberculture at the End of the Century*. New York: Grove Press.

Dewey, John. 1934. *Art as Experience*. New York: Capricorn Books.

Dickie, George. 1996. *The Century of Taste. The Philosophical Odyssey of Taste in the Eighteenth Century*. New York: Oxford University Press.

Diderot, Denis. 1986. *Jacques the Fatalist*. Translated by Michael Henry. New York: Penguin.

Dissanayake, Ellen. 1992. *Homo Aestheticus: Where Art Comes From and Why*. New York: The Free Press.

Dobrov, Gregory W. 2001. *Figures of Play. Greek Drama and Metafictional Poetics*. Oxford, U.K.: Oxford University Press.

Donadio, Rachel. 2005. "Truth is Stronger than Fiction." *The New York Times Book Review*. Sun. Aug. 28. [one page]

Donoghue, Denis. 2003. *Speaking of Beauty*. New Haven, CT: Yale University Press.

Douglas J. Yellowlees. 1994. "'How Do I Stop This Thing?' Closure and Indeterminacy in Interactive Narratives. In *Hyper/Text/Theory*. Edited by George P. Landow. Baltimore: The Johns Hopkins University Press.

Dover, Kenneth. 1993. *Frogs* by Aristophanes. Edited with Commentary by Kenneth Dover. Oxford, U.K.: Clarendon Press.

Dubois, Jacques. 1978. *l'Institution de la littérature*. Brussels: Editions Labor.

Dürrenmatt, Friedrich. 1964. *The Physicists*. Translated by James Kirkup. New York: Grove Press.

de Duve, Thierry. 1991. *Pictorial Monimalism. On Marcel Duchamp's Passage from Painting to the Readymade*. Translated by Dana Polan. Minneapolis: University of Minnesota Press.

Eagleton, Terry. 1990. *The Ideology of the Aesthetic*. Oxford: Basil Blackwell.

———. 2000. *The Idea of Culture*. Oxford, U.K.: Blackwell.

Eco, Umberto. 1989. *The Open Work*. Translated by Anna Cancogni. Cambridge, MA: Harvard University Press.

Edmundson, Mark. 1995. *Literature Against Philosophy, Plato to Derrida: A Defense of Poetry*. Cambridge, U.K.: Cambridge University Press.

Egbert, Donald Drew. 1970. *Social Radicalism and the Arts, Western Europe; A Cultural History from the French Revolution to 1968*. New York: Knopf.

Eichenbaum, Boris. 1965. *Russian Formalist Criticism. Four Essays*. Translated by Lee T. Lemon and Marion J. Reis. Lincoln: University of Nebraska Press.

Eisenstein, Elizabeth L. 1979. *The Printing Press as an Agent of Change: Communications and Cultural Transformation in Early-Modern Europe*. Cambridge, U.K.: Cambridge University Press.

Elliott, Emory, Louis Freitas Caton, and Jeffrey Rhyne Eds. 2002. *Aesthetics in a Multicultural Age*. Oxford, U.K.: Oxford University Press.

Ellis, John M. 1974. *The Theory of Literary Criticism*. Berkeley: University of California Press.

———. 1997. *Literature Lost: Social Agendas and the Corruption of the Humanities*. New Haven, CT: Yale University Press.

Esser, Andrea. Ed. 1995. *Autonomie der Kunst? Zur Actualität von Kant's Ästhetik*. Berlin: Akademie Verlag.

Fairchild, B. H. 1998. *The Art of the Lathe*. Farmington, ME: Alice James Books.

Feher, Ferenc, 1986. "The Pyrrhic Victory of Art in its War of Liberation: Remarks on the Postmodern Intermezzo." *Theory, Culture, and Society* 3: 2, 37–46.

Ferguson, Margaret. W. 1983. *Trials of Desire: Renaissance Defenses of Poetry*. New Haven, CT: Yale University Press.

Ferris, David S. 2000. *Silent Urns: Romanticism, Hellenism, and Modernity*. Stanford, CA: Stanford University Press.

Ferry, Luc. 1993. *Homo Aestheticus: The Invention of Taste in the Democratic Age*. Translated by Robert de Loaiza. Chicago: University of Chicago Press.

Fish, Stanley. 1980. *Is There a Text in This Class? The Authority of Interpretive Communities*. Cambridge, MA: Harvard University Press.

Fitzpatrick, Kathleen. 2008. "Obsolescence." *PMLA* 23: 3, 718–722.

Flaubert, Gustave. 1974. *Correspondance*, Vol. XIII, 1850–1859. Paris: Club de l'Honnête Homme.

———. 1976. *Bouvard and Pécuchet*. Translated by A. J. Krailsheimer. Harmdondworth, U.K.: Penguin.

Fluck, Winfried. 2002. "Aesthetics and Cultural Studies" In *Aesthetics in a Multicultural Age*. Edited by Emory Elliott, Louis Freitas Caton, and Jeffrey Rhyne. Oxford, U.K.: Oxford University Press.

Foer, Jonathan Safran. 2005. *Extremely Loud and Incredibly Close*. Boston: Houghton Mifflin.

Folsom, Ed. 2007. "Database as Genre: The Epic Transformation of the Archive." *PMLA* 122: 5, 1571–1579.

Fontius, Martin. 1977. "Productivkraftentfaltung und Autonomie der Kunst zur Ablösung ständiscer Voraussetzungen in der Literaturtheorie." In *Literatur im Epochenumbruch*. Edited by Günther Klotz, Winfried Schröder, and Peter Weber. Berlin: Aufbau Verlag.

Ford, Andrew. 2002. *The Origins of Criticism: Literary Culture and Poetic Theory in Classical Greece*. Princeton, NJ: Princeton University Press.

Forster, E. M. 1999. *Howards End*. New York: The Modern Library.

Foss, Michael. 1971. *The Age of Patronage: The Arts in Society 1660–1750*. London: Hamish Hamilton.

Foster, Hal. 1983. "Postmodernism: A Preface." In *The Anti-Aesthetic: Essays on Postmodern Culture*. Edited by Hal Foster. New York: The New Press, ix–xvi.

Fraser, Russell, 1970. *The War Against Poetry*. Princeton, NJ: Princeton University Press.

Friedman, Alan. 1966. *The Turn of the Novel*. New York: Oxford University Press.

Fukuyama, Francis. 1992. *The End of History and the Last Man*. New York: Free Press.

Gagnier, Regenia. 1994. "A Critique of Practical Aesthetics." In *Aesthetics and Ideology*. Edited by George Levine. New Brunswick, NJ: Rutgers University Press.

Gazda, Elaine K. 2002. "Beyond Copying: Artistic Originality and Tradition." In *The Ancient Art of Emulation*. Edited by Elaine K. Gazda. Ann Arbor: University of Michigan Press.

Gazzaniga, Michael S. 2008. *Human. The Science that Makes US Unique*. New York: Harper Collins.

Gillies, Mary Ann. 2007. *The Professional Literary Agent in Britain, 1880–1920*. Toronto: University of Toronto Press.

Gissing, George. 1891. *New Grub Street*. Harmondsworth: Penguin.

Glazer, Sarah. 2004. "An Idea whose Time has come back." *New York Times Book Review*, Dec. 5, p 31.

Gleizes, Albert and Jean Metzinger. 1964. "Cubism" In *Modern Artists on Art*. Edited by Robert L. Herbert. Englewood Cliffs, NJ: Prentice-Hall, 1–18.

Goodheart, Eugene. 1999. *Does Literary Studies Have a Future?* Madison: The University of Wisconsin Press.

Gordimer, Nadine. 1979. *Burger's Daughter*. London: Jonathan Cape.

Gourgouris, Stathis. 2003. *Does Literature Think? Literature as Theory for an Antimythical Age*. Stanford: Stanford University Press.

Grabes, Herbert. 1995. "Errant Specialisms: The Recent Historicist Turn Away From Aesthetics." *The Yearbook of Research in English and American Literature* 11, 159–172.

Graff, Gerald. 1987. *Professing Literature: An Institutional History*. Chicago: The University of Chicago Press.

Grass, Günter. 1966. *The Plebeians Rehearse the Uprising. A German Tragedy*. Translated by Ralph Manheim. New York: Harcourt, Brace & World.

Gray, Chris Hables. 2001. *Cyborg Citizen: Politics in the Posthuman Age*. New York: Routledge.

Greenberg, Clement. 1985. "Towards a Newer Laocoon." *Pollock and After: The Critical Debate*. Edited by Francis Frascina. New York: Harper and Row.

Haraway, Donna. 1991. *Simians, Cyborgs, and Women: The Reinvention of Nature*. New York: Routledge.

Hardy, Thomas. 1998. *Jude the Obscure*. London: Penguin.

Harlow, Barbara. 1987. *Resistance Literature*. New York: Methuen.

Hartman, Geoffrey. 2002. *Scars of the Spirit: The Struggle Against Inauthenticity*. New York: Palgrave Macmillan.

Hayles, N. Katherine. 1997. "Corporeal Anxiety in *Dictionary of the Khazars*: What Books Talk about in the Late Age of Print When They Talk about Losing Their Bodies." *Modern Fiction Studies* 43: 3, 800–820.

———. 1998. *How We Became Posthuman: Virtual Bodies in Cybernetics, Literature, and Informatics*. Chicago: The University of Chicago Press.

———. 2002. *Writing Machines*. Cambridge: MIT Press.

———. 2007. "Narrative and Database: Natural Symbionts." *PMLA* 122: 5, 1603–1608.

Hegel, G. W. F. 1975. *Aesthetics: Lectures on Fine Art*. Vol. I. Translated by T. M. Knox. Oxford, U.K.: Oxford University Press.

Heidegger, Martin. 1971. *Poetry, Language, Thought*. Translated by Albert Hofstadter. New York: Perennial Classics.

Herrnstein-Smith, Barbara. 1968. *Poetic Closure: A Study of how Poems End.* Chicago. The University of Chicago Press.

Hickey, Dave. 1997. *Air Guitar. Essays on Art and Democracy.* Los Angeles: Art Issues Press.

Hillis Miller, J. 1978. "The Problematic Ending in Narrative." *Nineteenth-Century Fiction* 33: 1, 3–7.

———. 1980. "The Figure in the Carpet." *Poetics Today* 1: 3, 107–118.

———. 2002. *On Literature.* London: Routledge.

Hohendahl, Peter Uwe. 1989. *Building a National Literature: The Case of Germany 1830–1870.* Ithaca, NY: Cornell University Press.

Hölderlin, Friedrich. 1946–1985. *Sämtlich Werke.* Edited by Friedrich Beissner. 8 Vols. Stuttgart: Kohlhammer.

———. 2004. *Poems and Fragments.* Translated by Michael Hamburger. London: Anvil Press.

Home, Henry, Lord Kames. 1867. *Elements of Criticism.* New York: S. Barnes & Co.

Horace. 1929. *Horace. Satires, Epistles, and Ars Poetica.* Translated by H. Rushton Fairclough. London: Heinemann.

Hubbard, Thomas K. 1991. *The Mask of Comedy. Aristophanes and the Intertextual Parabasis.* Ithaca, NY: Cornell University Press.

Huizinga, Johan. 1980. *Homo Ludens: A Study of the Play-Element in Culture.* London: Routledge.

Hume, David. 1963. *Essays: Moral, Political, and Literary.* Oxford, U.K.: Oxford University Press.

Hunter, Ian. 1988. *Culture and Government: The Emergence of Literary Education.* London: Macmillan.

Huyssen, Andreas. 1986. *After the Great Divide: Modernism, Mass Culture, Postmodernism.* Bloomington: Indiana University Press.

Ickstadt, Heinz. 2002. "Towards a Pluralist Aesthetics." In *Aesthetics in a Multicultural Age.* Edited by Emory Elliott, Louis Freitas Caton, and Jeffrey Rhyne. Oxford, U.K.: Oxford University Press.

Ioannou, Georgos. 1993. *Modern Greek Short Stories.* Edited by Nicholas Kostis. Athens: Odysseas Publications.

Iser, Wolfgang. 1974. *The Implied Reader: Patterns of Communication in Prose Fiction from Bunyan to Beckett.* Baltimore: Johns Hopkins University Press.

———. 1980. "Interaction between Text and Reader." *The Reader in the Text: Essays on Audience and Interpretation.* Edited by Susan R. Suleiman and Inge Crosman. Princeton, NJ: Princeton University Press.

———. 1993. *The Fictive and the Imaginary: Charting Literary Anthropology.* Baltimore: The Johns Hopkins University Press.

Izenberg, Gerald N. 1992. *Impossible Individuality: Romanticism, Revolution, and the Origins of Modern Selfhood, 1787–1802*. Princeton, NJ: Princeton University Press.

James, Henry. 1903. *The Better Sort*. Freeport, NY: Books for Libraries Press.

Jameson, Fredric. 1984. "Postmodernism, or the Cultural Logic of Late Capitalism." *New Left Review* 146: 53–92.

Jauss, Hans Robert. 1982. *Toward an Aesthetic of Reception*. Translated by Timothy Bahti. Minneapolis: University of Minnesota Press.

Jay, Martin. 2003. "Drifting into Dangerous Waters: The Separation of the Aesthetic Experience from Work. In *Aesthetic Subjects*. Edited by Pamela R. Matthews and David McWhitler. Minneapolis: University of Minnesota Press, 3–27.

Jehlen, Myra. 2008. *Five Fictions in Search of Truth*. Princeton, NJ: Princeton University Press.

Joughin, John J. and Simon Malpas. Eds. 2003. *The New Aestheticism*. Manchester, U.K.: Manchester University Press.

Joyce, James. 1976. *A Portrait of the Artists as a Young Man*. Harmondsworth, U.K.: Penguin.

———. 1977. *Stephen Hero*. London: Granada.

Joyce, Michael. 1987. "Afternoon, a Story." Watertown, MA: Eastgate Systems.

———. 1995. *Of Two Minds: Hypertext Pedagogy and Poetics*. Ann Arbor: University of Michigan Press.

———. 1997. "Nonce upon Some Times: Rereading Hypertext Fiction." *Modern Fiction Studies* 43: 3, 579–97.

———. 2000. *Othermindedness: The Emergence of Network Culture*. Ann Arbor: University of Michigan Press.

———. n.d. "Twelve Blue. Story in Eight Bars." (http://eastgate.com/TwelveBlue/sl5_9.html).

Jusdanis, Gregory. 1987. *The Poetics of Cavafy: Textuality, Eroticism, History*. Princeton, NJ: Princeton University Press.

———. 1991. *Belated Modernity and Aesthetic Culture: Inventing National Literature*. Theory and History of Literature 81. Minneapolis: University of Minnesota Press.

———. 2001. *The Necessary Nation*. Princeton, NJ: Princeton University Press.

———. 2002. "Greek Romanticism: A Cosmopolitan Discourse." In *Romantic Poetry*. Edited by Angela Esterhammer. Amsterdam: John Benjamins.

———. 2003. "World Literature: The Unbearable Lightness of Thinking Globally." *Diaspora* 12: 1, 103–130.

Kampf, Louis. 1969. "Notes Towards a Radical Culture." In *The New Left*. Edited by Priscilla Long. Boston: Extending Horizons Books, 420–34.

————. 1970. "The Trouble with Literature." *Change in Higher Education.* May/June, 27–40.

Kant, Immanuel. 1979. *The Conflict of the Faculties.* Translated by Mary J. Gregor. New York: Abaris Books.

————. 2000. *The Critique of Judgment.* Translated by J. H. Bernard. Amherst, NY: Prometheus Books.

————. 2001. *On History.* Translated by Lewis White Beck, Robert E. Anchor, and Emil L. Fackenheim. Upper Saddle River, NJ: Prentice Hall.

Kaufman, Robert. 2008. "Lyric Commodity Critique, Benjamin Adorno Marx, Baudelaire, Baudlaire, Baudlaire." *PMLA 123: 1,* 207–215.

Kay, Sarah. 2001. *Courtly Contradictions: The Emergence of the Literary Object in the Twelfth Century.* Stanford, CA: Stanford University Press.

Keats, John. 1966. *The Selected Poetry of Keats.* New York: New American Library.

Kerby, Anthony Paul. 1991. *Narrative and the Self.* Bloomington: Indiana University Press.

Kermode, Frank. 1966. *The Sense of an Ending: Studies in the Theory of Narrative Fiction.* New York: Oxford University Press.

Kernan, B. Alvin, 1987. *Printing Technology, Letters, and Samuel Johnson.* Princeton, NJ: Princeton University Press.

————. 1990. *The Death of Literature.* New Haven: Yale University Press.

Klee, Paul. 1964. "On Modern Art." In *Modern Artists on Art.* Edited by Robert L. Herbert. Englewood Cliffs, NJ: Prentice-Hall.

Kurzweil, Raymond. 1999. "The Future of Libraries." In *CyberReader.* Edited by Victor J. Vitanza. Boston: Allyn and Bacon.

Lacoue-Labarthe, Philippe and Jean-Luc Nancy. 1988. *The Literary Absolute*: *The Theory of Literature in German Romanticism.* Translated by Philip Barnard and Cheryl Lester. Albany: State University of New York Press.

Lambropoulos, Vassilis. 1988. *Literature as National Institution. Studies in the Politics of Modern Greek Criticism.* Princeton, NJ: Princeton University Press.

————. 1993. *The Rise of Eurocentrism: Anatomy of Interpretation.* Princeton, NJ: Princeton University Press.

Landow, George P. 1992. *Hypertext: The Convergence of Contemporary Theory and Technology.* Baltimore: The Johns Hopkins University Press.

Lanham, Richard A. 1993. *The Electronic Word: Democracy, Technology and the Arts.* Chicago: The University of Chicago Press.

Lansdown, Richard. 2001. *The Autonomy of Literature.* New York: St. Martin's Press.

Lessing, Gotthold Ephraim. 1965. *Laocoön: An Essay upon the Limits of Painting and Poetry.* Translated by Ellen Frothingham. New York: Noonday Press.

Levin, Susan B. 2001. *The Ancient Quarrel Between Philosophy and Poetry: Plato and the Literary Tradition*. Oxford, U.K.: Oxford University Press.

Levine, George. Ed. 1994. *Aesthetics and Ideology*. New Brunswick, NJ: Rutgers University Press.

Lewis, Philip. 2002. "Is Monographic Tyranny the Problem?" *PMLA* 117: 5, 1222–24.

———. 2004. "The Publishing Crisis and Tenure Criteria: An Issue for Research Universities?" *Profession 2004*. New York: MLA, 14–24.

Lodge, David. 2001. *Thinks: A Novel*. New York: Viking.

———. 2000. *Consciousness and the Novel: Connected Essays*. Cambridge, MA: Harvard University Press.

Loesberg, Jonathan. 2005. *A Return to Aesthetics: Autonomy, Indifference, and Postmodernism*. Stanford, CA: Stanford University Press.

Longinus. 1965. "On the Sublime." In *Classical Literary Criticism*. Edited and Translated by T. S. Dorsch. Baltimore: Penguin Books.

Lovell, Terry. 1987. *Consuming Fiction*. London: Verso.

Luhmann, Niklas. 2000. *Art as a Social System*. Translated by Eva M. Knodt. Stanford, CA: Stanford University Press.

Lukács, Georg. 1971. *The Theory of the Novel*. Translated by Anna Bostock. Cambridge MA: MIT Press.

MacIntyre, Alasdair. 1981. *After Virtue: A Study of Moral Theory*. London: Duckworth.

Maffesoli, Michel. 1996. *The Time of the Tribes: The Decline of Individualism in Mass Society*. Translated by Don Smith. London: Sage.

Malevich, Kasimir. 1964. "Suprematism." In *Modern Artists on Art*. Edited by Robert L. Herbert. Englewood Cliffs, NJ: Prentice-Hall.

Mallarmé, Stéphane. 1945. *Oeuvres Complètes*. Edited by H. Mondor and G. Jean-Aubry. Paris: Gallimard.

———. 1994. *Collected Poems*. Translated by Henry Weinfield. Berkeley: University of California Press.

Mann, Thomas. 1986. *Death in Venice*. New York: Buccaneer Books.

Manovich, Lev. 2001. *The Language of New Media*. Cambridge, MA: MIT Press.

Marcuse, Herbert. 1978. *The Aesthetic Dimension. Towards A Critique of Marxist Aesthetics*. Boston: Beacon Press.

Mariátequi, José Carlos. 1971. *Seven Interpretive Essays on Peruvian Reality*. Translated by Marjory Urquidi. Austin: University of Texas Press.

Martindale, Charles. 2005. *Latin Poetry and the Judgment of Taste: An Essay in Aesthetics*. New York: Oxford University Press.

Matthews, Pamela R., and David McWhitler. Eds. 2003. *Aesthetic Subjects*. Minneapolis: University of Minnesota Press.

Matz, Robert. 2000. *Defending Literature in Early Modern England: Renaissance Literary Theory in Social Context.* Cambridge, U.K.: Cambridge University Press.

Mauss, Marcel. 1990. *The Gift: The Form and Reason for Exchange in Archaic Societies.* Translated by W. D. Halls. New York: Norton.

McCormick, Peter J. 1990. *Modernity, Aesthetics, and the Bounds of Art.* Ithaca, NY: Cornell University Press.

McEwan, Ian. 2005. *Saturday.* New York: Doubleday.

McGann, Jerome. 2001. *Radiant Textuality: Literature after the World Wide Web.* New York: Palgrave.

McGowan, John. 2002. *Democracy's Children: Intellectuals and the Rise of Cultural Politics.* Ithaca, NY: Cornell University Press.

McKibben, Bill. 1989. *The End of Nature.* New York: Random House.

McLuhan, Marshall. 1962. *The Gutenberg Galaxy: The Making of Typographic Man.* Toronto: Toronto University Press.

Meikle, Graham. 2002. *Future Active: Media Activism and the Internet.* New York: Routledge.

Melville, Herman. 1962. *Billy Budd, Sailor.* Edited by Harrison Hayford and Merton M. Sealts Jr. Chicago: The University of Chicago Press.

Mendelsohn, Moses. 1929. *Schriften zur Philosophie und Ästhetik* II. Berlin: Akademie Verlag.

Messud, Claire. 2006. *The Emperor's Children.* New York: Vintage Books.

Mihajlović, Jasmina. 1998. "Milorad Pavić and Hyperfiction," *Review of Contemporary Literature* 18: 2, 214–20.

Miller, D. A. 1981. *Narrative and Its Discontents: Problems of Closure in the Traditional Novel.* Princeton, NJ: Princeton University Press.

MLA. 2002. "The Future of Academic Publishing." MLA Ad Hoc Committee on the Future of Academic Publishing. *Profession.* New York: MLA, 171–86.

Moritz, Karl Philipp. 1962. *Schriften zur Ästhetik und Poetik.* Tübingen: Max Niemeyer.

Morrisson, Mark S. 2001. *The Public Face of Modernism: Little Magazines, Audiences, and Reception, 1905–1920.* Madison: The University of Wisconsin Press.

Moses, Daniel David. 1900. *The White Line.* Saskatoon: Fifth House Publishing.

Mukarovsky, Jan. 1970. *Aesthetic Function, Norm and Value as Social Facts.* Translated by Mark E. Suino. Ann Arbor: Michigan Slavic Contributions.

Murray, Janet H. 1997. *Hamlet on the Holodeck: The Future of Narrative in Cyberspace.* New York: The Free Press.

Murrell, Mary. 2001. "Is Literary Studies Becoming Unpublishable?" *PMLA* 116: 2, 394–96.

Nehamas, Alexander. 2000. "The Return of the Beautiful: Morality, Pleasure and The Value of Uncertainty." *The Journal of Aesthetics and Art Criticism.* 58: 4, 393–403.

———. 2007. *Only a Promise of Happiness: The Place of Beauty in a World of Art.* Princeton, NJ: Princeton University Press.

Neithammer, Lutz. 1992, *Posthistoire: Has History Come to an End?* Translated by Patrick Camiller. London Verso.

Nelson, Theodor Holm. 1992. *Literary Machines.* Sausalito, CA: Mindful Press.

Neruda, Pablo. 1970. *Selected Poems.* Translated by Anthony Kerrigan, W. S. Merwin, Alastair Reid, and Nathaniel Tarn. Boston: Houghton Mifflin.

Newcomb, John Timberman. 2004. *Would Poetry Disappear? American Verse and the Crisis of Modernity.* Columbus: The Ohio State University Press.

Ngugi Wa Thiong'o. 1972. *Homecoming. Essays on African and Caribbean Literature, Culture, and Politics.* London: Heinemann.

———. 1981. *Writers in Politics.* London: Heinemann.

Nussbaum, Martha C. 1995. *Poetic Justice: The Literary Imagination and Public Life.* Boston: Beacon Press.

O'Brien, Tim. 1990. *The Things They Carried. A Work of Fiction.* Boston: Houghton Mifflin.

Odin, Jaishree K. 1997. "The Edge of Difference: Negotiating Between the Hypertextual and the Postcolonial." *Modern Fiction Studies.* 43: 3, 598–630.

Ong, Walter J. 1982. *Orality and Literacy: The Technologizing of the Word.* London: Methuen.

Pamuk, Orhan. 2004. *Snow.* Translated by Maureen Freely. New York: Knopf.

Parini, Jay. 2008. *Why Poetry Matters.* New Haven, CT: Yale University Press.

Paulson, William. 2001. *The Literary Culture in a World Transformed: A Future for the Humanities.* Ithaca, NJ: Cornell University Press.

Pavić, Milorad. 1989. *Dictionary of the Khazars: A Lexicon Novel.* Translated by Christina Pribićević-Sorić. New York: Vintage International.

———. 1998. "The Beginning and the End of Reading—The Beginning and the End of the Novel," *Review of Contemporary Literature* 18: 2, 142–46.

Pessoa, Fernando. 1982. *Selected Poems.* Translated by Jonathan Griffin. Harmondsworth: Penguin.

———. 1986. *Poems of Fernando Pessoa.* Translated by Edwin Honig and Susan M. Brown. San Francisco. City Lights.

Plato. 1945. *The Republic of Plato.* Translated by Francis MacDonald Cornford. New York: Oxford University Press.

———. 2005. *Phaedrus.* Translated by Christopher Rowe. London: Penguin.

Plotinus. 1992. *The Enneads.* Translated by Stephen MacKenna. Burdett, NY: Larson Publications.

Postman, Neil. 1985. *Amusing Ourselves to Death. Public Discourse in the Age Show Business*. New York: Viking.

Pound, Ezra. 2003. *Poems and Translations*. New York: Library of America.

Ramadanović, Petar. 1994. "Language and Crime in Yugoslavia: Milorad Pavić's *Dictionary of the Khazars*." In *Regionalism Reconsidered: New Approaches to the Field*. Edited by David Jordan. New York: Garland Publishing.

Reiss, Timothy J. 2002. *Against Autonomy: Global Dialectics of Cultural Exchange*: Stanford, CA: Stanford University Press.

Rheingold, Howard. 2000. *The Virtual Community: Homesteading on the Electronic Frontier*. Rev. ed. Cambridge, MA: The MIT Press.

Rich, Frank. 2006. *The Greatest Story Ever Sold. The Decline and Fall of Truth from 9/11 to Katrina*. New York: Penguin Press.

Riffaterre, Michael. 1973. "Interpretation and Descriptive Poetry: A Reading of Wordsworth's 'Yew Trees.'" *New Literary History*, 229–56.

Rilke, Rainer Maria. 1955. *Duino Elegies and the Sonnets of Orpheus*. Translated by A. Poulin Jr. Boston: Houghton Miffllin.

Robbe-Grillet, Alain. 1960. *In the Labyrinth*. Translated by Richard Howard. New York: Grove Press.

Robinson, Douglas. 2008. *Estrangement and the Somatics of Literature. Tolstoy, Shklovsky, Brecht*. Baltimore: The Johns Hopkins University Press.

Roche, Marc William. 2004. *Why Literature Matters in the 21st Century*. New Haven, CT: Yale University Press.

Rosenberg, Harold. 1972. *The De-Definition of Art*. New York: Collier Books.

Ryle, Martin, and Kate Soper. 2002. *To Relish the Sublime? Culture and Self-Realization in Postmodern Times*. London: Verso.

Scarry, Elaine. 1999. *On Beauty and Being Just*. Princeton, NJ: Princeton University Press.

Schiller, Friedrich. 1901. *Wallenstein: Ein Dramatisches Gedicht*. Edited by W. H. Carruth. New York: Hendry Holt.

———. 1966. *Naïve and Sentimental Poetry and On the Sublime*. Translated by Julius A. Elias. New York: Frederick Ungar.

———. 1967. *On the Aesthetic Education of Man. In a Series of Letters*. Edited and Translated by Elizabeth M. Wilkinson and L. A. Willoughby. Oxford, U.K.: Oxford University Press.

Schlegel, Friedrich. 2001. *On the Study of Greek Poetry*. Translated by Stuart Barnett. Albany: State University of New York Press.

Schmitt, Carl. 1986. *Political Romanticism*. Translated by Guy Oakes. Cambridge, MA: MIT Press.

Schulte-Sasse, Jochen. 1989. "The Prestige of the Artist under Conditions of Modernity." *Cultural Critique* 12, 83–100.

Schwartz, Delmore. 1978. *In Dreams Begin Responsibilities and Other Stories.* New York: New Directions Publishing.

Schwarz, Heinrich. 1985. *Art and Photography: Forerunners and Influences.* Layton, UT: Peregrine Smith Books.

Sharpe, Kevin, and Steven N. Zwicker. Eds. 1998. *Refiguring Revolutions: Aesthetics and Politics from the English Revolution to the Romantic Revolution.* Berkeley: University of California Press.

Sheehan, James J. 2000. *Museums in the German Art World. From the End of the Old Regime to the Rise of Modernism.* Oxford, U.K.: Oxford University Press.

Shelley, Percy Bysshe. 1890. *A Defense of Poetry.* Edited by Albert S. Cook. Boston: Ginn & Com.

Shiner, Larry. 2001. *The Invention of Art: A Cultural History.* Chicago: University of Chicago Press.

Shklovsky, Victor. 1965. *Russian Formalist Criticism. Four Essays.* Translated by Lee T. Lemon and Marion J. Reis. Lincoln: University of Nebraska Press.

Sidney, Philip. 1965. *An Apology for Poetry or The Defense of Poetry.* Edited by Geoffrey Shepherd. London: Thomas Nelson & Sons.

Siebers, Tobin. 1998. "Kant and the Politics of Beauty." *Philosophy and Literature* 22:1, 31–50.

Simmel, Georg. 1968. *The Conflict in Modern Culture and Other Essays.* Translated by K. Peter Etzkorn. New York: Teachers College Press.

Simpson, David. 1995. *The Academic Postmodern and the Rule of Literature; A Report on Half-Knowledge.* Chicago: The University of Chicago Press.

Siskin, Clifford. 1998. *The Work of Writing: Literature and Social Change in Britain, 1700–1830.* Baltimore: The Johns Hopkins University Press.

Soderholm, James. Ed. 1997. *Beauty and the Critic: Aesthetics in an Age of Cultural Studies.* Tuscaloosa: The University of Alabama Press.

Spengler, Oswald. 1926–28. *The Decline of the West.* Trans. Charles Francis Atkinson. New York: Knopf.

Steiner, Wendy. 2001. *Venus In Exile: The Rejection of Beauty in Twentieth-Century Art.* New York: The Free Press.

Stevens, Wallace. 1951. *The Necessary Angel. Essays on Reality and the Imagination* New York: Vintage.

Stolnitz, Jerome. 1961a. "On the Origins of 'Aesthetic Disinterestedness.'" *The Journal of Aesthetics and Art Criticism* 20: 2, 130–43.

———. 1961b. "On the Significance of Lord Shaftsbury in Modern Aesthetic Theory." *The Philosophical Quarterly* 11: 43, 99–113.

Stoppard, Tom. 1982. *The Real Thing.* New York: Samuel French.

———. 2001. *Voyage.* New York: Grove Press.

Strauss, Richard. 1942. *Capriccio. A Conversation Piece for Music in One Act.*

Tarada, Rei. 2008. "After the Critique of Lyric." *PMLA* 123: 1, 195–200.

Taylor, Mark C. 2001. *The Moment of Complexity: Emerging Network Culture.* Chicago: The University of Chicago Press.

Taylor, Mark C., & Esa Saarinen. 1994. *Imagologies: Media Philosophy.* New York: Routledge.

Todorov, Tzvetan. 1980. "Reading as Construction." In *The Reader in the Text.* Edited by Susan R. Suleiman and Inge Crosman. Princeton, NJ: Princeton University Press.

Tolstoy, Leo. 1978. *The Portable Tolstoy.* Translated by Aylmer Maude. Edited by John Bayley. Harmondsworth, U.K.: Penguin Books.

Tuman, Myron C. 1992. *Word Perfect: Literacy in the Computer Age.* London: Palmer Press.

Turgovnick, Marianna. 1981. *Closure in the Novel.* Princeton, NJ: Princeton University Press.

Turner, Fred. 2006. *From Counterculture to Cyberculture: Stewart Brand, the Whole Earth Network, and the Rise of Digital Utopianism.* Chicago: University of Chicago Press.

Turner, Mark. 1996. *The Literary Mind.* New York: Oxford.

Turner, Victor. 1967. *The Forest of Symbols. Aspects of Ndembu Ritual.* Ithaca, NY: Cornell University Press.

———. 1969. *The Ritual Process. Structure and Anti-Structure.* Ithaca, NY: Cornell University Press

Updike, John. 1973. *Pigeon Feathers and Other Stories.* New York: Knopf.

Valéry, Paul. 1972. *Leonardo, Poe, Mallarmé.* Translated by Malcolm Cowley and James R. Lawler. *The Collected Works of Paul Valéry.* Vol. 8. Princeton, NJ: Princeton University Press.

Vattimo, Gianni. 1988. *The End of Modernity: Nihilism and Hermeneutics in Post-Modern Culture.* Translated by John R. Snyder. Cambridge, U.K.: Polity Press.

———. 2008. *Art's Claim to Truth.* Translated by Luca D'Isanto. Edited by Santiago Zabala. New York: Columbia University Press.

Vesna, Victoria. Ed. 2007. *Database Aesthetics: Art in the Age of Informational Overflow.* Minneapolis: University of Minnesota Press.

Vizyenos, Georgios. 1988. *My Mother's Sin and Other Stories.* Translated by William F. Wyatt Jr. Hanover, NH: University Press of New England.

Wachtel, Andrew. 1997. "Postmodernism as Nightmare: Milorad Pavić's Literary Demolition of Yugoslavia." *The Slavic and East European Journal* 41: 4, 627–44.

Wagner, Richard. 1980. "Die Meistersinger von Nürnberg." In *The Opera Libretto Library.* New York: Avenel Books.

Wall-Romana, Christophe. 2005. "Mallarmé's Cinepoetics: The Poem Uncoiled by the Cinématographe, 1893–98." *PMLA* 120: 1, 128–47.

Wartofsky, Marx. 1980. "Art, Artworlds, and Ideology." *Journal of Aesthetics and Art Criticism* 38: 239–47.

Weber, Bruce. 2004. "Fewer Noses Stuck in Books in America, Survey Finds." *New York Times*. July 8, B1, B4.

Weber, Max. 1946. *From Max Weber: Essays in Sociology*. Translated by H. H. Gerth and C. Wright Mills. New York: Oxford University Press.

Weiss, Peter. 1965. *The Persecution and Assassination of Jean-Paul Marat as Performed by the Inmates of the Asylum of Charenton Under the Direction of the Marquis de Sade*. Translated by Geoffrey Skelton. New York: Atheneum.

Wellek, René. 1970. *Discriminations*. New Haven, CT: Yale University Press.

Wells, H. G. 1996. *The Time Machine and The Island of Doctor Moreau*. New York: Oxford University Press.

Welty, Eudora. 1980. *The Collected Stories*. San Diego: Harcourt Brace Jovanovich.

White, Hayden. 1987. *The Content of Form: Narrative Discourse and Historical Representation*. Baltimore: The Johns Hopkins University Press.

Wilde, Oscar. 1945. *Intentions*. London: Unicorn Press.

———. 1974. *The Picture of Dorian Gray*. London: Oxford University Press.

Williams, Raymond. 1977. *Marxism and Literature*. Oxford: Oxford University Press.

Wilson, Edmund. 1931. *Axel's Castle: A Study in the Imaginative Literature of 1870–1930*. New York: Charles Scribner's Sons.

Winckelmann, Johann Joachim. 1968. *History of Ancient Art*. Translated by Alexander Gode. New York: F. Ungar Pub. Co.

———. 1987. *Reflections on the Imitation of Greek Works in Painting and Sculpture*. Translated by Elfriede Heyer and Roger C. Norton. La Salle, IL: Open Court.

Wolff, Tobias. 2003. *Old School. A Novel*. New York: Knopf.

Wood, James. 2008. *How Fiction Works*. New York. Farrar, Straus & Giroux.

Woodmansee, Martha. 1984. "The Interest in Disinterestedness: Karl Philipp Moritz and the Emergence of the Theory of Aesthetic Autonomy in Eighteenth-Century Germany." *Modern Language Quarterly* 17: 3, 22–47.

Woodring, Carl. 1999. *Literature: An Embattled Profession*. New York: Columbia University Press.

Wright, James. 1971. *Collected Poems*. Middletown, CT: Wesleyan University Press.

Wright, Richard. 1937. *Black Boy*. New York: Harper and Row.

Yeats, William Butler. 1962. *Selected Poems and Two Plays*. New York: Collier.

Zammito, John. H. 1992. *The Genesis of Kant's Critique of Judgment*. Chicago: University of Chicago University Press.

Zei, Alki. 1991. *Achilles' Fiancée.* Translated by Gail Holst-Warhaft. Athens: Kedros.

Zill, Nicholas and Marianne Winglee. 1989. *Who Reads Literature? The Future of the United States as a Nation of Readers.* Washington, DC: Seven Locks Press.

Index

Adorno, Theodor, 53, 55, 70
Aeschylus, 79–82
Aestheticism, 27–28, 49–52
Aristophanes, 73–77
Aristotle, 21
Art, attack on 20; biological origins of, 16–17; and capitalism 45–46; as communal practice, 39–42; and dedifferentiation 28–29; definition of, 7; and performance, 64–65; and play, 17, 64–65; and politics 52–53, 70–71; rise of, 37, 42–43; as self-institution 64–66; and simulation, 64–70; social diffusion of 30–33
Autonomy, 7

Balzac, Honoré de, 46–47
Book, end of , 101–107
Brecht, Bertolt, 23. 128n4

Carver, Raymond, 67–69
Cavafy, Constantine P., 49–50; 119–120
Cheever, John, 61–62

Danto, Arthur C., 13, 20
Database aesthetic, 101–102
Dürrenmatt, Friedrich, 86–87

Fairchild, B. H., 1, 10
Forster, E. M. 25–26

Gissing, George, 47–48
Grass, Günter, 84–86

Hardy, Thomas, 24–25
Hegel, G. W. F., 13
Hypertext, and end of books, 108–110; and print, 107–108

Joyce, James, 27, 35, 58, 116–117, 124n17
Joyce, Michael, 110–113

Kant, Immanuel, 14; and aesthetics, 37–39; and art as communal practice, 39–42; and university, 39–40

Literature, attack on, 21–22; and autonomy, 1; biological origins of, 16–17, 127n7; death of, 12, 115; defense of, 22–23; relevance of, 11; and society 24–29; and teaching, 11–12
Luhmann, Niklas, 7, 66, 121n1, 126n1

Mallarmé, Stéphane, 90–91
Moses, Daniel David, 78–79

Open text, 113–115

Pamuk, Orhan, 97–99
Parabasis, 3–4; and Aristophanes'
    "Acharnians," 73–74; and
    Aristophanes' "Frogs," 74–77;
    as metaphor, 79
Pavić, Milorad, 101–105
Plato, 21
Poetry, defense of, 22–23
Pound, Ezra, 117–118

Romanticism, 54–55
Russian Formalism, 58–59

Schiller, Friedrich, 22, 34, 43–44
Schwartz, Delmore, 88–90

Shelley, Percy Bysshe, 23
Sidney, Philip, 8, 23
Simulation, 3
Strauss, Richard, 87–88, 99–100,
    131n21

Updike, John, 62–63

Vattimo, Gianni, 30–31
Vizyenos, Georgios, 95–97

Wagner, Richard, 117–118
Weiss, Peter, 82–84
Welty, Eudora, 59–61
Winckelmann, Johann Joachim, 33
Wright, Richard, 69–70

Zei, Alki, 92–95